Animal Farm

GEORGE ORWELL

Guide written by

John Mahoney

A *Letts* EXPLORE **Literature Guide**

First published 1994
Reprinted 1998
This edition revised by Ron Simpson

Letts Educational
Aldine House
Aldine Place
London W12 8AW
0181 740 2266

Text © John Mahoney and Stewart Martin 1994

Typeset by Jordan Publishing Design

Self-test questions devised by Sandra Lissenden

Text design Jonathan Barnard

Cover and text illustrations Hugh Marshall

Graphic illustration Ian Foulis and Associates, Barbara Linton

Design © BPP (Letts Educational) Ltd

Acknowledgements
The author and publishers are grateful to the Estate of Sonia Brownell Orwell for permission to quote from *Animal Farm* by George Orwell, published by Secker and Warburg Ltd.

Examination questions reproduced by kind permission of the Northern Examination and Assessment Board.

The answers supplied to the Exam Board questions are solely the responsibility of the author, and are not supplied or approved by the Exam Boards.

British Library Cataloguing in Publication Data
A CIP record for this book is available from the British Library

ISBN 1 85758 260 8

Printed and bound in Great Britain
Ashford Colour Press, Gosport, Hampshire

Letts Educational is the trading name of BPP (Letts Educational) Ltd

■ Contents

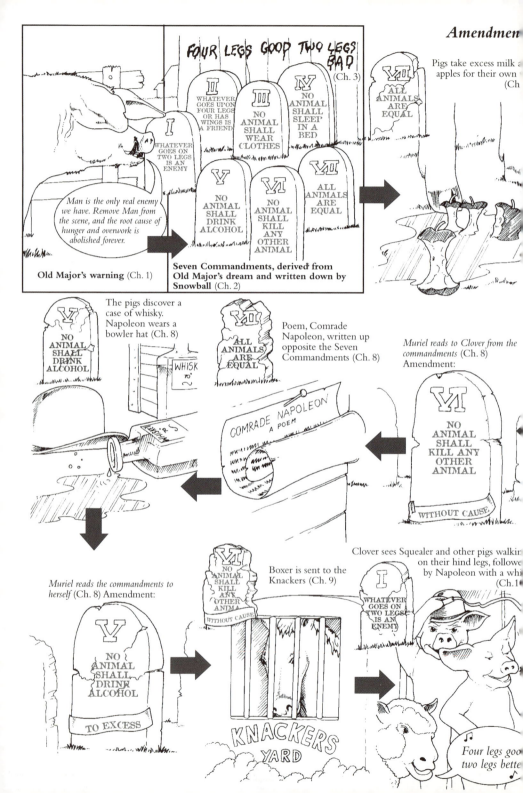

FOUR LEGS GOOD TWO LEGS BAD (Ch. 3)

II WHATEVER GOES UPON FOUR LEGS OR HAS WINGS IS A FRIEND

III NO ANIMAL SHALL WEAR CLOTHES

IV NO ANIMAL SHALL SLEEP IN A BED

I WHATEVER GOES ON TWO LEGS IS AN ENEMY

V NO ANIMAL SHALL DRINK ALCOHOL

VI NO ANIMAL SHALL KILL ANY OTHER ANIMAL

VII ALL ANIMALS ARE EQUAL

Man is the only real enemy we have. Remove Man from the scene, and the root cause of hunger and overwork is abolished forever.

Old Major's warning (Ch. 1)

Seven Commandments, derived from Old Major's dream and written down by Snowball (Ch. 2)

VII ALL ANIMALS ARE EQUAL

Pigs take excess milk a apples for their own (Ch

V NO ANIMAL SHALL DRINK ALCOHOL

The pigs discover a case of whisky. Napoleon wears a bowler hat (Ch. 8)

WHISK

VII ALL ANIMALS ARE EQUAL

Poem, Comrade Napoleon, written up opposite the Seven Commandments (Ch. 8)

Muriel reads to Clover from the commandments (Ch. 8) Amendment:

COMRADE NAPOLEON A POEM

VI NO ANIMAL SHALL KILL ANY OTHER ANIMAL

WITHOUT CAUSE

Muriel reads the commandments to herself (Ch. 8) Amendment:

V NO ANIMAL SHALL DRINK ALCOHOL

TO EXCESS

VI NO ANIMAL SHALL KILL ANY OTHER ANIMA

WITHOUT CAUSE

Boxer is sent to the Knackers (Ch. 9)

KNACKERS YARD

Clover sees Squealer and other pigs walkir on their hind legs, followe by Napoleon with a whi (Ch. 1

I WHATEVER GOES ON TWO LEGS IS AN ENEMY

Four legs goo two legs bette

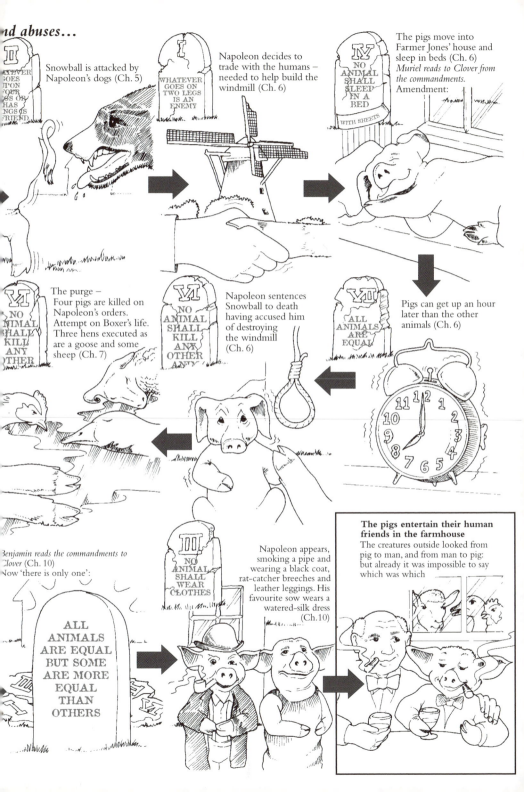

...and abuses...

Snowball is attacked by Napoleon's dogs (Ch. 5)

(II) WHATEVER GOES ON TWO LEGS IS AN ENEMY

Napoleon decides to trade with the humans – needed to help build the windmill (Ch. 6)

(I) WHATEVER GOES ON TWO LEGS IS AN ENEMY

The pigs move into Farmer Jones' house and sleep in beds (Ch. 6)
Muriel reads to Clover from the commandments.
Amendment:

(IV) NO ANIMAL SHALL SLEEP IN A BED WITH SHEETS

The purge –
Four pigs are killed on Napoleon's orders. Attempt on Boxer's life. Three hens executed as are a goose and some sheep (Ch. 7)

(V) NO ANIMAL SHALL KILL ANY OTHER

Napoleon sentences Snowball to death having accused him of destroying the windmill (Ch. 6)

(VI) NO ANIMAL SHALL KILL ANY OTHER ANIMAL

(VI) ALL ANIMALS ARE EQUAL

Pigs can get up an hour later than the other animals (Ch. 6)

Benjamin reads the commandments to Clover (Ch. 10)
Now 'there is only one':

(III) NO ANIMAL SHALL WEAR CLOTHES

Napoleon appears, smoking a pipe and wearing a black coat, rat-catcher breeches and leather leggings. His favourite sow wears a watered-silk dress (Ch.10)

ALL ANIMALS ARE EQUAL BUT SOME ARE MORE EQUAL THAN OTHERS

The pigs entertain their human friends in the farmhouse
The creatures outside looked from pig to man, and from man to pig: but already it was impossible to say which was which

■ Plot synopsis

The animals of Manor Farm, mistreated by the farmer Mr Jones, are told of a dream by Old Major, a well-respected boar. Old Major's dream is of a time when animals will be free to control their own destinies without interference or exploitation by man. Old Major dies, but his dream is kept alive by the pigs Napoleon and Snowball. One night, driven by anger and hunger, the animals, led by Napoleon and Snowball, rise up and drive Farmer Jones and his wife from the farm.

The animals rename the farm Animal Farm and create Seven Commandments by which they agree to be ruled. Snowball is active in committees and in helping to educate the animals. Napoleon takes on the education of a litter of puppies, isolating them from the other animals.

Conflict occurs between Snowball and Napoleon and it becomes obvious that Napoleon has ambitions to rule alone. The animals labour together, taking inspiration from the titanic efforts of the horse Boxer, who adopts as his motto: 'I must work harder'. They find learning very hard work and most of them give up.

Neighbouring farmers attempt to win the farm back but are beaten off. The final conflict between Napoleon and Snowball comes when elections are held. Snowball is accused of betraying the revolution and Napoleon sets his 'secret police', the dogs he has been 'educating', onto Snowball, who has to flee for his life.

Once he has undisputed control of Animal Farm, Napoleon proves an even more brutal ruler than Farmer Jones. The Seven Commandments are re-written and discarded, one by one. Finally all that is left is a statement that 'All animals are equal, but some animals are more equal than others'. Napoleon and his pig henchmen open up trade with the human beings and the story ends with Napoleon and the other pigs playing cards with the local farmers in Mr Jones' farmhouse. The starving animals, looking in through the windows, are unable to distinguish the men from the pigs. Old Major's dream has turned into a nightmare.

■ Who's who in *Animal Farm*

This is a brief overview of the main characters. Use it as a starting point for your own character studies. For each aspect of character mentioned, look in the text for evidence to support or contradict both the views expressed here and your own views.

Note the animal characteristics which Orwell uses in presenting the inhabitants of *Animal Farm*; they add a sense of 'caricature' to the story.

Napoleon

In many ways, Napoleon represents Stalin, the tyrannical ruler of the USSR after the Russian Revolution. However, as his name suggests, Napoleon is made up of characteristics which dictators usually share. One criticism of this characterisation might be that Napoleon is unbelievable as a character because he has no redeeming features. But, bearing in mind why Orwell wrote this book, it is perhaps wrong to expect the characters to be rounded or fleshed out. The book is a political satire or allegory, and it is a feature of such writing that events are simple and characters two-dimensional in order to put the author's message across in the most effective way.

Furthermore, though Napoleon may have no redeeming features morally, he has qualities which make him stand out from the other pigs. He and Snowball are described as 'pre-eminent among the pigs' before the Rebellion: what qualities caused his pre-eminence? Napoleon succeeds in building up support from the animals even before the machine of propaganda (Squealer and Minimus) and terror (the dogs) is in place: how does he do it?

Animal Farm focuses on Napoleon's rise to power. His character gradually changes for the worse as his power over the animals increases. Lacking the idealism of Old Major or Snowball, Napoleon is a political opportunist. His ruthlessness and determination more than make up for his lack of intellect – as is the case with many dictators.

Snowball

Snowball

If *Animal Farm* is taken as an allegory of the Russian Revolution, Snowball represents Trotsky. Like Trotsky, Snowball is a brilliant speaker and is the intellectual inspiration for the revolution. He works sincerely and selflessly for the benefit of all the animals. Orwell makes fun of some of Snowball's behaviour, but nevertheless clearly intended Snowball to represent a hopeful alternative to Napoleon.

Snowball's character is a study of a sincere revolutionary who is out-manoeuvred by a more ruthless and cunning opponent. Snowball's ideas are misappropriated and his character vilified by Napoleon in order to deceive and betray the animals.

Old Major

Old Major represents both Marx and Lenin in that he introduces the fundamental theories and ideals on which the revolution is to be based. One Marxist theory expressed is that an animal's labour has more intrinsic value than is required for its own needs. The surplus is stolen by parasitic man. There is a nice irony here in the way in which Napoleon eventually steals the results of the animals' labour for his own needs. It is also ironic that, under Mr Jones' authority, the farm was less productive than it is after the revolution and consequently there was less for Mr Jones to steal.

The 'Lenin' side of Old Major's character is shown in the part of his speech which reduces complex philosophy to fundamental propositions or maxims which everyone can understand. There is also a parallel between the homage paid to Old Major's skull by the animals and the exhibition of Lenin's embalmed body in Red Square, Moscow.

Of course, you will have noticed that Old Major's identification with Lenin is not complete: he dies before the Rebellion; Lenin led the October Revolution. In that respect Snowball (mainly identified with Trotsky) takes on the Lenin role.

Squealer

Squealer

Squealer is one of the four pig founders of the new society formed after the revolution. Like Napoleon, he is an opportunist. It is not clear how much of his propaganda is the work of Napoleon and the other pigs, and how much of it is his own. He has an uncanny knack of choosing the right moments for his explanations of events.

Squealer is presented as a small fat pig, nimble in mind and body. He thrives with the growth of the new society and achieves high status within it. He plainly enjoys his work, which is essential to Napoleon's success. At the very first mention of Squealer it is said that he could 'turn black into white', and this is his job as head of Napoleon's propaganda machine. He is the equivalent of the vast media machine that presented the Government's version of events in the USSR, as in all dictatorships.

Squealer deals in half-truths, omissions and plain lies. He feeds the workers illusions that help them to endure their harsh existence. His purpose is to stifle public understanding or awareness of real events and so forestall any challenge to the pigs' power.

Boxer

Boxer

Boxer is an enormously strong horse upon whom the work of the farm, and therefore its survival, depends. He is a gentle giant, and his philosophy is simple, based on the dignity of labour. He is exploited by whoever runs the farm and, because of his crucial importance in the farm work and his lack of any sort of critical perception, he unwittingly contributes to the exploitation of the other animals.

Boxer represents the ordinary worker, decent, honest and essential to the success of any social system. Such a worker is inevitably exploited under a dictatorship or totalitarian regime. Even after his death, Boxer's favourite slogans, 'work harder' and 'Napoleon is always right', are used cynically to control the other animals. He never realises that the ideals of the revolution are being corrupted, but at least he is spared the sight of pigs and men becoming indistinguishable in the final scenes.

Consider how Boxer changes during the course of the story. Note one change in his attitude towards hurting others: compare, for example, the incident where he injures the stable-boy with the time when the dogs attack him. It is possible to criticise Boxer for being unimaginative in his response to what is happening around him, but perhaps Orwell uses his character to warn that ceaseless hard work can have a dulling effect on the mind and spirit. Boxer's experiences under the regime at Animal Farm show what can happen when the actions of those in power are accepted unquestioningly.

Benjamin

Benjamin is a cynic – one who doubts the sincerity or ability of those around him. He is also sceptical – he doubts the truth of many theories or facts. Benjamin learns to read, but he consistently refuses to put this skill to any useful purpose. Only at the final collapse of Animalism ('All animals are equal, but some are more equal than others') does Benjamin agree to read the Commandment(s) to the animals: by then Muriel, the usual reader, is dead. Benjamin can be seen as representing the uninvolved intellectual who achieves nothing, despite his wisdom, and he is the great survivor: 'the oldest animal on the farm' in Chapter 1, still there at the end. Do not, however, forget his loyalty to Boxer and his frantic attempts to save him.

Orwell emphasises that Benjamin never laughs, though traditionally donkeys are known for their braying. Perhaps this is a comment on the joyless nature of many of man's political ideals?

Clover

Clover is the maternal figure of the farm. Her good sense is sound if limited, and complements Boxer's qualities of simple goodness and strength. More than any other, she is the animal who displays sympathy and kindness. She is disturbed in a way that the others are not by the outrages which take place on the farm. But she is a survivor and is a source of comfort and strength for the oppressed animals.

Dogs and sheep

The dogs and the sheep are each treated as a group, not individuals, and each group reveals qualities traditionally associated with the animal. Think of guard-dogs or hounds for the dangerous qualities of the dogs and add in a twisted version of canine loyalty. Sheep, of course, are proverbial for being easily led and not thinking for themselves.

Dogs and sheep clearly represent two important groups in Soviet society (or any dictatorship): the secret police suppressing opposition through fear and intimidation, and the easily-manipulated, slogan-chanting masses.

Muriel

Muriel, the goat, is linked with Benjamin from the first chapter. They are similar in their literacy and lack of political involvement. However, there is no suggestion that Muriel understands the significance of what she reads: unlike Benjamin, she accepts that she must have forgotten what was written on the wall. Also, of course, she is always ready to read the latest version to the other animals: this is her main role in the novel.

Mr Jones

Mr Jones is the cause of the rebellion at the farm in the same way that Czar Nicholas II was, in very simple terms, the cause of the Russian Revolution. Mr Jones has fallen on hard times, and so there is some excuse for his drunkenness, but his brutality to and neglect of the animals are less excusable. He is the most fully developed of the human characters but is still little more than a stereotype.

Pilkington and Frederick

Pilkington and Frederick represent types of man, but also different nations. Pilkington is a gentleman farmer whose farm, Foxwood, is badly managed because he spends all his time enjoying country sports. Frederick is aggressive, efficient and extremely cruel to the animals on his farm: unlike Pilkington who is merely neglectful.

The more obvious link is between Frederick and Germany: Frederick the Great was a famous Prussian king and 'Pinchfield' (i.e. 'steal land') is a reference to Hitler's territorial ambitions. Pilkington, therefore, must represent the Allies: perhaps Britain and France, 'Foxwood' sounding British, with its suggestions of hunts in the countryside. Note the way that Napoleon sides with first one, then the other. This is the equivalent of Stalin's treaties with, in turn, Nazi Germany and the Western Allies.

■ Themes and images in *Animal Farm*

Revolution and corruption

Revolution and corruption

'Animalism', the revolutionary doctrine adopted by the animals, is based on Old Major's teaching in the same way that communism was originally based on the teachings of Karl Marx. However, communism can mean different things to different people and in different societies. Different communist countries are as much influenced by individual leaders and particular national characteristics as they are by political doctrines.

It is a mistake to consider *Animal Farm* as just a satire on communism. Animalism is interchangeable with a range of 'isms': fascism, socialism, conservatism, flat-earthism and so on, in that it is not so much the doctrine that is corrupt or faulty, as the individuals in power. Old Major, despite his good intentions, fails to notice a crucial point: whilst his ideas may be sound and his intentions high-principled, corrupt individuals will find ways to twist them to their own purposes. What happens in *Animal Farm* shows this. Corruption means moral deterioration, which is exactly what happens to Old Major's ideals once Napoleon puts them into practice.

Animal Farm plots Napoleon's corruption and his decline into most of the seven deadly sins: pride, lust, envy, gluttony, anger, laziness, and desiring others' goods. Identify the particular occasion when Napoleon indulges himself in each of these sins. Note the circumstances and any reasons or excuses he gives to justify his actions.

Note instances of corruption as they occur in the story, and trace the way in which corruption gradually affects every animal, both those who suffer because of it, and those who gain from it. Look, for example, at how clothing creates identity and influences personality. The vanity and superficiality of Mollie and of Napoleon's favourite sow are exemplified by the clothes they choose. Mr Jones and Napoleon are linked by their wardrobe; Napoleon's vanity is illustrated in his 'black coat, ratcatcher breeches, and leather leggings'. Food and drink, basic currencies of life, recur as images of corruption. Alcoholic drink is a symbol of corruption and when the pigs drink it, it shows their moral squalor.

Communication

Communication

Throughout the story, events are rewritten according to the prevailing political needs of the pigs. This perhaps criticises nostalgia, or the tendency to romanticise the past. In *Animal Farm*, the pigs manage to turn nostalgia on its head by referring to the bad old days of life under Mr Jones. They make them seem worse than they actually were in order to make their own brutal excesses seem less shocking to the animals. The control of books, of thought, and of history is a vital weapon in the armoury of authoritarian political systems.

The constitution of *Animal Farm* is contained in Seven Commandments. These are slowly corrupted over the course of a few years, and their original meaning is changed. Eventually, none of Old Major's revolutionary principles is left and the remaining commandment, which is the creation of the corrupt pigs, is simply a licence for the pigs to do as they please.

As you read the novel, take note of the process by which the high ideals of Old Major are distilled and translated into the Seven Commandments, then gradually changed and finally obliterated. Perhaps this parallels the way the Ten Commandments, on which much of our own society is based, have been watered down or reinterpreted over time.

Orwell was conscious of the interaction between opinion and language. He said of *Animal Farm* that it was, 'The only one of my books I really sweated over'. He said his aim was 'to fuse political and artistic purpose into one whole.' In that sense, he was himself engaged in a kind of propaganda exercise, wanting his readers to learn from the story.

Propaganda is the spreading of a particular idea, doctrine, policy, or opinion, with the intention of influencing people.

How were Boxer, Clover and the other animals so deceived that they elevated Napoleon to the status of a demi-god? To achieve this, the pigs used the tools of dictatorship; the manipulation of emotions such as fear, anger and patriotism; the giving of misinformation; and the control of basic necessities like food and education, which can be used to 'persuade' individuals to take the propagandist's point of view.

All Squealer's speeches are propaganda, as are Napoleon's and the poetry of Minimus. So, less obviously, are Moses the raven's. Read and study these speeches carefully, and identify the methods of persuasion used.

Note Snowball's attempts to educate the animals. Not long ago, many people in this country could not read and write. Only at the beginning of this century was it accepted that education is a human right. The power of the written word and development of mass communications mean that it is essential for any would-be dictator or power-hungry politician to gain control of the media. The failure to use one's mental capacity, by allowing others to think for you and by being, like Muriel the Goat, satisfied with the 'rubbish heap' as the main source of news, is a disservice not only to oneself but to the whole of society. Note how the animals fail to respond to Snowball's attempts to educate them and how they suffer for this in the long term.

Examiner's tip icon

This icon is used to draw attention to a section of the **Text commentary** that is particularly relevant to the titles considered in **How to write an examination essay**. Each time it is used, a note adds a comment or piece of advice.

Animal Farm, satire and the Russian Revolution

A Fairy Story?

Animal Farm is described on the title page as 'a fairy story'. You may well wonder why: there are no fairies in it and, though the story is not naturalistic, it evidently deals with the real world of ideas and politics. Perhaps George Orwell wanted to disarm criticism, to pretend that it was a children's book, because he encountered much opposition to the political message (see below). Or perhaps it was just an ironic joke. There are, in fact, several terms that you should consider in relation to *Animal Farm*, and these are discussed below.

- An animal fable is an ancient form of story (associated mainly with Aesop) in which animals behave in a way that is half-human and half-animal. Usually they adopt a human version of their traditional animal qualities: consider whether Orwell does this in such cases as the pigs or the sheep. The animals can speak, but their actions are more animal-like than, say, Pooh or Toad of Toad Hall. Above all, the animal fable points a moral and teaches a lesson.

- Satire is criticism using oblique, frequently amusing, means. Though often humorous, satire can be quite vicious and the main intent is to ridicule: many satirists would claim that they wish to reform vices by this ridicule. You may well have come across examples of satire on television. Orwell ridicules the pursuit of power by placing it in a farmyard.

- An allegory is a story which conceals its main meaning beneath the surface of a quite different narrative. Many people interpret parables in the Bible as allegories. The essential feature of an allegory is that each main person or event in the surface story should have an equivalent in the hidden story. You will find it possible to make this connection in *Animal Farm*.

George Orwell (1903–1950)

Animal Farm, written in 1943–44 and published in 1945, is now considered George Orwell's finest novel. Although he wrote fiction successfully in the 1930s, his other outstanding novel, *1984*, also an attack on totalitarian regimes like the USSR, was not published until 1949. The best known of Orwell's books before *Animal Farm* are sociological and political non-fiction and reflect his own life and views very strongly.

Born Eric Blair, he was educated at Eton and took up a conventional colonial career with the Indian Imperial Police in Burma. He found this sort of work intolerable and left the force in 1927: his life there is charted in *Burmese Days* (1935). For many years he lived somewhere near the bread-line, earning modest sums as a journalist and a private tutor, taking casual jobs and attempting to run a village store. Two startling accounts of the life of the poor belong to this period: *Down and Out in Paris and London* (1933) and *The Road to Wigan Pier* (1937). Despite ill-health, Orwell volunteered in 1936 to fight in the Spanish Civil War against Franco's Fascists: his experiences, which included being wounded, are recounted in *Homage to Catalonia* (1938).

The Soviet Union supported the Communist opposition to Franco and Orwell was always a left-wing thinker and an opponent of privilege, so we might expect him to take a favourable view of the Soviet Union, as many in Britain did at the time. However, he was a passionate believer in justice, freedom and equality, and far too honest to pretend that Stalin's Soviet Union encouraged these. In Spain he had joined (by mistake, as much as anything) a Trotskyite group, POUM, which the Russian-controlled Communists suppressed, though they were, in a sense, 'on the same side'. He was appalled when Stalin and Hitler signed a non-aggression pact in August 1939 which encouraged Hitler's invasion of Poland.

By the time that Orwell came to write *Animal Farm*, the Soviet Union had joined the war against Nazi Germany and patriotic Britons were not expected to criticise our brave allies. He was not surprised when his regular publisher, Victor Gollancz, refused the book: in a letter to a friend in February 1944 he wrote, 'it is so not OK politically that I don't feel certain in advance that anyone will publish it.' By the time Secker and Warburg published it in August 1945, the war was over and suspicion between the West and the USSR had returned.

Animal Farm deals with how people behave before, during and after revolutions in general, and Orwell makes general political points, but there is no doubt that he is specifically attacking the Soviet Union. In a preface to the Ukrainian edition in 1947, he wrote, 'And so for the past ten years I have been convinced that the destruction of the Soviet myth was essential if we wanted a revival of the Socialist movement.' He went on to write, 'I proceeded to analyse Marx's theory from the animals' point of view', though it was necessary in the novel to alter the exact chronology of events. The final scene with the farmers, he explained, was based on an event that was taking place as he began writing the book: the Tehran conference of 1943 between Roosevelt, Churchill and Stalin: 'I personally did not believe that such good relations would last long; and, as events have shown, I wasn't far wrong'.

The following brief account of some of the major events in the Russian Revolution and the first 25 years of Communist rule will show how precise is the satire in *Animal Farm*.

The Russian Revolution and Stalin's USSR

The Russian Revolution in 1917 was really two revolutions, like the Rebellion and the Battle of the Cowshed, although in Russia different people took part. The February Revolution was a spontaneous response to suffering and hunger (and also to Russian disasters in World War I) and led to a moderate government. The October Revolution established the Bolsheviks (Communists) in power, with Lenin supreme and Trotsky and Stalin both prominently placed. As with the Battle of the Cowshed, the October Revolution occurred after conservative forces attempted to re-capture St. Petersburg; Trotsky, like Snowball, distinguished himself by his generalship. By the death of Lenin (1924), the Union of Soviet Socialist Republics (USSR) was firmly established and the leadership was the subject of a power struggle between Stalin and Trotsky (Napoleon and Snowball).

One of the major differences between the two was that Trotsky believed in international co-operation of workers, leading to world revolution, and Stalin advocated 'socialism in one country'. This is reflected in *Animal Farm*, as are the stages by which Trotsky became a non-person (literally being air-brushed out of history by doctoring photographs) and was exiled from the Soviet Union in 1929. He was eventually murdered in Mexico in 1940.

The old Russian Empire had been largely agricultural, with a large peasant population. The Soviet Union moved to increasing industrialisation and vast collective farms: peasants who opposed collectivisation (joining small farms together under state control) were treated like the hens who opposed proposals to take their eggs. So the Knoll represents Russian feeling for the land, for Mother Russia, and the windmill represents industrialisation.

An over-simplified, but basically accurate, examination of Soviet life before the Second World War reveals three further tendencies. The early free debates of political ideas were succeeded by a totalitarian dictatorship banning free speech: "totalitarian" means centrally controlled by only one party. Industrial progress was charted in a series of Five-Year Plans, the successes of which were exaggerated, but which became more realistic and more aimed at international trade as time went on. Finally, all hints of opposition were ruthlessly suppressed: the secret police (OGPU) and show trials awaited Stalin's enemies. You will find equivalents of all these in *Animal Farm*.

In the late 1930s conflict between Nazi Germany and the West became increasingly likely. The Soviet Union attempted to play one against the other, as Napoleon does with Frederick and Pilikington. The pact between Germany and the USSR, agreed in 1939, was suddenly broken when Hitler's troops invaded Russia in 1941. The destruction of the country was savage, but, with heroic resistance, notably at the siege of Stalingrad, the Soviets forced a German retreat the following year: paralleled in the Battle of the Windmill. The Soviet Union was thus drawn into war on the side of the Western Allies.

■ Text commentary

Chapter 1

Old Major summons the farm animals to a meeting in the big barn after Mr Jones, the farmer and owner of Manor Farm, has gone to bed. At the meeting, Old Major tells the animals of his dream of a Utopian society, free from parasitic Man. Old Major tells them to prepare for a rebellion emphasising the need for unity and warning against adopting Man's ways once they have won their freedom. He teaches them the song 'Beasts of England', which describes an ideal society.

Mr Jones

Like the other human characters, Mr Jones plays a minor role in the book. His brutality to the animals is the reason they plan revolution. Later, the threat of his return to Animal Farm helps reinforce the pigs' authority over the other animals. Mr Jones' drunkenness is paralleled later by the pigs' over-indulgence in drink.

Note that Mr Jones has no redeeming features. Having introduced him as a drunken, neglectful farmer, the narrative concentrates on the animals. Mrs Jones is introduced with even fewer words; asleep and snoring next to her worthless husband, she seems, by association, to be equally worthless.

Old Major

Old Major has had a dream important enough to be shared with the other farm animals. From his appearance and because of his past history it is obvious that Old Major is greatly admired by the other animals, so they will listen to what he has to say with respect. The name Major itself implies some seniority and rank.

Revolution and corruption

The first meeting called by Old Major establishes the characters of the story and sets the scene for the revolution. Significantly, Old Major's vision for the future has its origins in a dream. However it is one thing to have a dream and quite another thing to see it translated into reality. It is ironic that an animal who has apparently been well cared for, should be the one who dreams of freedom from human oppression. Like Karl Marx, who spent years in study at the British Museum perfecting his theories, Old Major has had more time to think than most of the animals. It could be argued that, as things later turn out, Old Major's real legacy to the animals only leads them into greater oppression, long after he has died peacefully in his sleep. Would you agree?

Optimism and unity

The mood of the first meeting is optimistic. Compare this to the animals' despondency at the final meeting when they are subject to the oppression of their fellow animals, the pigs.

Introducing the animals

The sheep are briefly introduced here. They have no individual identity and merely follow whoever directs them; they behave as one would expect a flock of sheep to behave. Consider whether they merely reflect the feelings and behaviour of the majority. Note that because of their docile nature they play a crucial part in the story.

Boxer

Boxer the horse has two companions: Clover, a mare, and Benjamin, a donkey. Boxer and Clover are like a long-married couple. Consider the extent to which they are a caricature of 'Mr and Mrs Average' who do not think for themselves, preferring instead to place blind trust in the decisions of those they believe to be their natural superiors. Clover is established as a gentle and maternal character. Her most prominent quality is sympathy, in contrast to the callousness of the pigs. As you read the story, consider whether she has too limited a perspective on events and whether she could have contributed something more practical or useful than sympathy and understanding to the animals' cause.

Benjamin

Benjamin is cynical about the events both before and after the revolution. He has misgivings about Old Major's dream and about the pigs' later conduct, but does he actually do anything to prevent the abuses that follow? Would it be fair to accuse him of failing the revolution in this respect, as he is conscious of what is going on? Compare Benjamin with Old Major, who is idealistic and impractical. Benjamin makes cryptic comments about events as they unfold. Despite his exterior cynicism, he is deeply devoted to Boxer. The unspoken nature of his affection makes it the more convincing, especially when compared with the pigs' frequent, insincere declarations of good intent later in the story.

Consider the differences in character and appearance between the two mares, Mollie and Clover. Mollie enters 'mincing daintily'. She is 'chewing at a lump of sugar', indicating her priorities: she desires the 'sugary', non-essential things of life. Her vanity is seen in the way she shows off her red ribbons.

Traditionally, ravens are sinister birds associated with misfortune. They make unusual pets. But note this raven's name – Moses. In Christian art, the raven is often a symbol of God's bountiful nature. Take note of the part Moses plays in the story.

Old Major speaks

Old Major indicates that he is nearing the end of his life. His age and maturity give his words great importance. He graphically describes the life of a farm animal. He uses plain, simple language, with repetition and short sentences that are like slogans: 'no animal in England is free'. This an effective way of communicating with the farm animals. They find long sentences difficult to follow and their concentration-span is short.

Communication

Old Major asks a series of questions asking why the animals lead such appalling lives. This a useful technique for a speaker to use, as he can provide the right questions and then supply the answers he wants. Thus the animals are not required to think for themselves, merely to agree with what he says. Compare Old Major's public-speaking techniques with those used by Squealer later on.

Old Major moves towards the crux of his speech – the parasitic nature of Man. Man lives off animals but gives them virtually nothing in return. Old Major shows sympathy for the animals' plight and provides examples of Man's exploitation. References to Clover's lost foals and the stolen milk and eggs are calculated to arouse the listening animals' indignation.

Old Major then describes in horrific detail the deaths the animals will suffer, particularly Boxer. Think about what eventually happens to Boxer. Why is his fate ironic, in the light of Old Major's words here?

This speech is the equivalent of the Communist Manifesto by Karl Marx and Friedrich Engels. Man represents the capitalist system, exploiting the labour of the animals/working-classes. The last sentences of the Communist Manifesto are, 'The workers have nothing to lose ... but their chains. They have a world to gain. Workers of the world, unite!' If you read Major's speech carefully, you will find sentences stressing the need for unity and many which emphasise the animals' state of slavery ('chains').

Chapter 1 is, in a sense, the prelude to the main story, but you must be clearly aware of the first principles which Animal Farm gradually betrays. Major's speech is important to the understanding of all three essay titles considered on pages 62–65.

Misleading arguments

Old Major aims to sow the seeds of revolution, recognising it will take several generations to achieve his idea of a utopian society. He warns the animals to beware of persuasive but misleading arguments. Ironically, this first warning is the one they most quickly forget. Things might have turned out differently if they had taken it to heart. Old Major's use of very simple slogans, so that even the dullest animal can grasp his message, is effective but dangerous. The slogans are open to various interpretations, as will later be shown.

The scuffle between the dogs and the rats emphasises the difference

Revolution and corruption

between what Old Major says about unity, and the reality of the animals' natural aggression towards each other. Old Major offers a simple concept: all animals are friends and Man is the common enemy. He forgets that some animals naturally prey upon others. Most important of all, he ignores the fact that some animals are cleverer than others. Old Major's idealism fails to take account of the practical difficulties involved in creating a new society.

Prophecies of the future

Old Major warns the animals that once Man is conquered, the animals must be careful not to copy Man's vices. This is ironic when set against the later behaviour of the pigs and some of the other animals. Try to decide for yourself which of Old Major's ideals are tossed aside later, and note when each happens. Old Major's vision of an ideal animal society is, to some extent, founded on naive, sweeping generalisations and over-confident predictions. Is it a fault or a strength that he sees situations in simple terms?

'Beasts of England'

To conclude his speech, Old Major sings a song, 'Beasts of England'. It has simple, emotional appeal and describes a joyous future for the animals, stressing the positive aspects of their new life. Its simple rhythm and rhyme pattern make it easy to remember and it becomes the animals' revolutionary anthem. 'Beasts of England' represents the first great song of Communism, 'The International', calling on workers of all lands to rise up. Note that it involves all animals, not just those of Animal Farm. You should enjoy the mix of seriousness and humour in the song. Its tune ('something between *Clementine* and *La Cucuracha*') is the first gently mocking joke: see how many lines you can find which are faintly ridiculous.

It is important to your understanding of the novel to appreciate fully the mood of excitement and joy at the outset. Animalism (like Russian Communism) is a response to a real need which makes the betrayals by Napoleon and Stalin all the more shameful.

Chapter 2

Old Major dies, but plans for the rebellion continue. The pigs convert Old Major's ideas into a social system called Animalism which, with some difficulty, they teach to the other farm animals. One day, Mr Jones neglects to feed the animals and, quite spontaneously, they turn on him and his men and drive them from the farm. They destroy all traces of Man's oppression, turn the farmhouse into a museum, write Seven Commandments on the barn wall and rename the farm Animal Farm. While Snowball and the animals get in the harvest, Napoleon takes the cows' milk for himself and the other pigs.

Death of the dreamer

Old Major dies peacefully in his sleep. How might this death be significant

Revolution
and corruption

for one who has communicated a vision based on a dream? He is buried near the orchard, perhaps suggesting that his ideas might grow in a fruitful way.

The pigs begin to instruct and organise the animals, preparing them for rebellion. The three pigs, Napoleon, Snowball and Squealer are described in some detail. Napoleon, 'a fierce-looking Berkshire boar', is named after one of Europe's most famous revolutionaries, who turned a popular uprising into a dictatorship. Snowball is described as 'more vivacious' than Napoleon, but he was considered to have less 'depth of character'. His name implies that he will 'melt away' or be overshadowed by Napoleon. Squealer is introduced as a 'brilliant talker'. His name perhaps implies treachery: 'squealer' is slang for someone who will tell secrets under pressure.

Practical problems

Napoleon, Snowball and Squealer translate Old Major's vision into a work-

Communication

able system, but encounter difficulties in communicating it to the animals. Note the stupidity, self-interest and apathy of the various animals, mirroring aspects of modern society.

Snowball is the brains behind the principles of Animalism. He tries to explain to Mollie that ribbons and sugar are not as important as oats and hay and must be sacrificed if the revolution is to succeed. It is clear that Mollie is not the stuff from which revolutionaries are made!

Moses arrives

Moses the raven was absent during Old Major's assembly in Chapter 1. He is now introduced as Mr Jones' special pet. Consider the implications of his simplistic notion of 'life hereafter'. Why should we worry about things now when such a wonderful life awaits us after death? The author is using Moses as a vehicle to criticise established churches and their teachings. Though the pigs ridicule Moses' ideas here, notice how they later turn them to their advantage. What is the significance of Moses' claim that animals go to Sugarcandy Mountain when they die? Is this promise of 'heaven' nothing more than a bribe to ensure obedience?

Note the satire on the Christian church contained in the character of Moses. His name is that of the prophet who saved God's people from the slavery of the Egyptians, yet Moses' advice to the animals is that they should continue to live in slavery under Mr Jones. There were very strong ties between the Czars and the Russian Orthodox Church. Each had an interest in preserving tradition and was seen as the enemy of change. Through Moses the Russian Orthodox Church in particular, and Christianity in general, is attacked for serving the wishes of the ruling classes. The Christian church's Communion (wafers of bread and wine) is parodied by the crusts of bread soaked in beer which Mr Jones fed his pet.

Boxer and Clover

It is important for the pigs to win the support of Clover and Boxer, as the other animals have great respect for these two animals. Unfortunately, Boxer and Clover lack the intelligence or wit to think for themselves.

Reaping the harvest

Mr Jones' harvest was ready for reaping in more ways than one: he reaps the rewards of getting drunk and neglecting his animals. Note, however, that although the secret meetings helped to put the animals in the right frame of mind for revolution, when the rebellion happens it is a spontaneous response to anger and hunger.

Revolution and corruption

The first battle

Compare the lightness of the first skirmish with the intensity of the later battles. No one is hurt, and the humans look comical rather than tragic as they take to their heels. Mr Jones is expelled quickly and easily by the united animals.

Symbols of oppression

The cruel and humiliating methods which Mr Jones used to keep the animals in submission – nose-rings, dog chains, and so on – are easy to identify. Keep this in mind as the story develops, and consider how the pigs manage to keep the animals enslaved without such devices: psychological 'chains' can be quite as effective as physical ones, though the dogs, in particular, later exert their own physical menace.

Snowball

Boxer

Snowball has already expressed his disapproval of ribbons and the vanity which goes with them. Here he develops his ideas more fully, declaring them the mark of the hated humans and saying that all animals should go naked. Note how some animals are suddenly making rules for the other animals. There has been no discussion, merely the issue of a decree.

Boxer decides to give up his straw hat — not worn for reasons of vanity, but to keep away flies in summer — as a demonstration of his wholehearted support for the revolution. It is typical of Boxer's lack of self-esteem that, under Snowball's influence, he equates his working hat with Mollie's silly ribbons. This is an early indication of Boxer's naivety and readiness for self-sacrifice, and contrasts with the calculated self-interest with which the pigs later go about their work.

Napoleon provides

It is Snowball who leads the animals to destroy the hated symbols of oppression. Napoleon assumes the role of provider by giving food to the animals. Which action are the animals more likely to remember? This is how Napoleon gets a head start in establishing superiority.

Napoleon

Consider the implications of Napoleon's position as the provider of food so soon after the revolution. There is no random looting of the foodstore, as might have been expected, but rather a careful allocation of corn and biscuits under the supervision of Napoleon. What does this tell you about the animals' mood at this point in the story?

In this chapter Orwell succeeds in presenting a common mood of euphoria for the animals whilst indicating the different ways in which they will develop: Snowball and Napoleon already see different demands of power; Boxer and Molly have opposite views of obedience.

The Knoll

The animals are overjoyed as they view the farm, now under their control, from the top of the Knoll. Remember this scene later, when the Knoll becomes the setting for confessions and executions. Compare the words and movements of the animals on the different occasions they visit the Knoll during the story.

Snowball and Napoleon investigate the farmhouse

Snowball and Napoleon take the lead in entering the farmhouse. From what you know of him, how characteristic is this of Snowball? And how typical of

Napoleon is it to take the lead in this way? Does this quality in Napoleon change during the book?

Mollie has to be cautioned about her fondness for ribbons. Compare this to the way the animals reverentially bury the hams. There is evidently a huge difference in the attitudes and hopes of the different animals. In contrast to the respect shown to the hams, Boxer kicks in the barrel of beer, seen as the cause of much suffering. Keep this in mind when the pigs later indulge their appetite for food and drink in the farmhouse. Here, the pigs decree that no animal shall ever live in the farmhouse.

The entry into the farmhouse is Orwell's version of the famous attack on the Czar's Winter Palace in Petrograd. This happened during the October Revolution, but this is one of several alterations to the order of events. The mixture of wonder and disgust at the sights within links the two events.

Importance of literacy

Consider the importance which Snowball gives to literacy. How different

Communication

might life have been for the animals if they could have learned to read and write? Do you think Napoleon really wanted all the animals to become literate?

In any modern society, a literate, concerned and involved population is the key to democracy. When a large section of the community is illiterate, it finds it difficult to understand politicians' words, and democratic institutions face real danger from ambitious men.

Manor Farm becomes *Animal Farm*

Napoleon leads the way to Manor Farm gate, but it is Snowball who paints in the name Animal Farm. Notice that, although Napoleon gives the orders, it is Snowball who has the ability to write.

Place-names were significant in the Russian Revolution. For instance, the city of St Petersburg had been re-named Petrograd in 1914 to sound less German and more Russian. After the Revolution it was again re-named: Leningrad. Ironically, it has recently returned to the name St Petersburg, just as in the closing pages of *Animal Farm* the name reverts to Manor Farm.

The Seven Commandments

At the next meeting, Snowball and Napoleon introduce the basic tenets of

Revolution
and corruption

Animalism and tell the animals that they are to learn to read and write. At this stage, are the two leaders working together in harmony, or is Napoleon merely biding his time?

Snowball writes up the Seven Commandments himself. Do you think that it is likely that he also composed them? The Commandments establish the foundation for post-revolutionary life at Animal Farm. Be aware of how and at what point in the story these Commandments are gradually changed as the pigs gain power. What effect do these changes have on the animals' lives? What weaknesses are there in the animals' society which enable the pigs to change the original Commandments?

For many essays you will need to remember and understand the Seven Commandments. They express the ideals of Animalism codified (compare with the original principles of Communism) and their destruction provides a framework for the plot and a yard-stick for judging characters.

Squealer helps to fix the Seven Commandments on the big barn wall. Later in the novel, Squealer will not be content with holding the paint pot; he will actually do the writing himself, altering the Commandments to convey whatever meaning the pigs regard as helpful to them at the time.

Squealer

An unalterable law

Snowball summarises the ideal of Animalism into Seven Commandments and

Revolution
and corruption

writes them up on the barn wall for all to read and observe as 'an unalterable law by which all animals on Animal Farm must live for ever after'. Although the Seven Commandments are intended as guidelines and as a safeguard for the constitution of Animal Farm, they are later exploited and used to manipulate the working animals. Is the key to their failure the facts that the animals fail to learn to read and have short memories?

The revolutionary ideals of Old Major find their expression in the Seven Commandments. As each Commandment is successively betrayed, so are his original ideals. What parallels can you see here between the Seven Commandments and the Ten Commandments of Christian belief? Do you think the author is suggesting that, just as the pigs of Animal Farm interpret their Commandments to suit them, so do Christians with theirs, and man with any kind of law?

Communication

Already a gap is widening between 'the cleverer ones' and the other animals in their understanding of the Seven Commandments. One of the key insights in Animal Farm is that the language used by governments is sometimes remote from the language of the average man. Snowball does his best to simplify the system of Animalism into the Seven Commandments and various slogans, but this will not work if the animals are illiterate, are too busy with other matters, are cynical, or are simply uninterested in their own welfare.

The changes made to the Commandments reflect the weakening of Old Major's original ideals and the animals' decline into a way of life worse than anything they experienced under Mr Jones.

Napoleon shows his priorities

In calling for the harvest to be gathered quickly, Snowball shows his practical nature. Compare his attitude with that of Napoleon, who takes charge of the milk – the first hint of his greed. Mr Jones mixed surplus milk in the hens' mash. This is a practice that Napoleon will not follow. Napoleon's greed here is an early indication of how much worse life will be for the animals under his regime.

The animals leave the meeting, inspired by their new life. Are there any indications that the new regime is already under attack from within?

Chapter 3

A bumper harvest is gathered in record time and the summer is a happy one. All the animals work hard, especially Boxer. On Sunday mornings, a flag of green, with a hoof and horn symbol, is raised and the week's work is planned. Snowball and Napoleon are the leaders, but always disagree with each other. Snowball sets up various committees and organises classes to teach reading and writing. The sheep learn a new slogan and keep repeating it. Napoleon takes a litter of puppies and educates them in isolation. The pigs take the apple crop, saying it is necessary for 'brain-work'.

Working together

The introductory paragraphs of this chapter indicate how the revolution might have worked. Almost every animal unselfishly and willingly gives of its best. There is total co-operation between them, and not a grain is stolen. As yet, there is nothing sinister in the fact that they are working under the direction of the pigs. Notice that the animals work just as hard now as they do later under Napoleon's oppressive leadership. Why then does Napoleon treat the animals the way he does? When he gains power, the fear of losing it makes him brutal and oppressive.

Human or animal workers?

This chapter is an excellent example of Orwell's skill in applying human activities to animal abilities. As far as possible the animals do things that animals can do and the details are convincing, touching and amusing. The ducks and hens, for instance, carry 'tiny wisps of hay in their beaks'. Later in the chapter you will find animal equivalents of human activities: reading and forming committees (with wonderful names like The Wild Comrades' Re-education Committee). See how many humorous examples of this balance between animal and human you can enjoy.

The workers make their contribution

Boxer

Boxer is essential to the success of the farm, and has such pride in his work that he earns universal respect. Despite these good qualities, he is flawed: his view of life is conditioned by a few simple slogans. By limiting himself in this way, he becomes the unwitting tool of Napoleon's corrupt ambitions to take complete control of the farm.

Consider how lazy and deceitful Mollie is when work needs to be done. She is at best a passenger, if not a positive hindrance in the new society. She is an example of someone who would be of little practical use to any social system. The cat is another example of a parasite, feeding on the fruits of others and contributing nothing.

Benjamin

Benjamin remains stubbornly unmoved by the revolution in a way which suggests he has low expectations of the new Animal Farm, unlike Boxer who expects much. Is Benjamin wiser than the other animals in his view of the future, or is his attitude another reason why the revolution fails? Is it reasonable for him to take a realistic, even cynical view of events? Is he right to stand back from trying to influence them?

The flag of the revolution

The green flag with hoof and horn is the exact equivalent of the USSR flag: the red flag with hammer and sickle (representing industrial and agricultural workers). You will notice in Animal Farm, as in real life, many examples of the symbolic use of flags, decorations and anthems.

Signs of disagreements

Revolution and corruption

Napoleon and Snowball, the two leaders, are in open disagreement. Disagreements of this kind do not occur once Snowball has left the farm. Why? Note that the disagreements are not constructive, but occur because different points of view are held by different animals. This is sometimes referred to as 'confrontation politics'. Consider how effective such politics are in serving the mass of the population. Are there examples of it in our own political system? For all their shortcomings, open debates on policy and planning at least take place – they no longer will once Napoleon is in sole command. Any open system of government, however confrontational, self-centred and power-seeking, is better than one where no discussion at all takes place.

Characters' responses to the new situation are already being characterised by typical behaviour or slogans: Snowball and Napoleon's disagreements, Boxer's 'I will work harder', Squealer's 'Surely ... no one ... wants to see Jones come back?' and the sheep's 'Four legs good, two legs bad'.

Committee man

Snowball is always busy with schemes that are intended to benefit the animals,

but from which they seem to gain little. There seems to be a gap between Snowball's ideals and the other animals' simple aspirations. Squealer seems to have a better understanding of his audience: his later comment: 'surely none of you want Jones back' is a persuasive argument.

The news that almost every animal on the farm is now literate to some degree should give Snowball great satisfaction, but the ability to read is not sufficient in itself. If what we read is garbled and worthless and adds nothing to our knowledge and understanding, what is the value of being literate?

The list detailing which animals can read, how well, and to what uses they

Communication

put their reading satirises not only Animal Farm's society, but our own as well. The pigs learn easily and make the most of their learning, but in a self-centred way. The dogs read fairly well, but have no interest in broadening their minds, displaying what will later appear as a dangerous tendency to unthinking loyalty and obedience. Muriel the goat uses a rubbish heap as her source of reading. Benjamin simply refuses to use his ability to read, thus wasting his talents. Clover and Boxer try hard to learn, but fail. Mollie thinks of nothing except her own ridiculous vanity. Look around your own circle of friends and see if you can identify similar characters.

Animal understanding

Communication

Clover shows herself to be a little more intelligent than Boxer, but not as physically strong. She occasionally shows some perception about the events at Animal Farm, but not enough to see through the treachery of the power-hungry pigs. Boxer and Clover's difficulties in mastering the simple concept of the alphabet discourages them from learning more.

Undeterred by the failure of some of the animals to learn to read and write, Snowball cleverly reduces the principles of Animalism to a slogan that even the dimmest animal can understand: 'Four legs good, two legs bad'. Unfortunately, the sheep take this simple saying too much to heart and later repeat it mindlessly to frustrate Snowball's good intentions.

Napoleon's guard dogs

The dogs are introduced as puppies, which Napoleon takes away and educates

in isolation. Dictators are not the only people who recognise the value of early indoctrination. Any nation's future lies in the hands of its children, and the better-educated – in the widest sense – that they are, the better it is for the nation. However, do not forget that Napoleon's plans for the puppies have little to do with enlightenment. Napoleon indoctrinates them: he teaches them to think the way he wants them to. Compare the experiences of the puppies with the elitist upbringing of the young pigs later in the book.

The puppies later become Napoleon's bodyguard and chase Snowball from the farm. Napoleon plans this from the start, since the birth of the litter coincides with Napoleon's quarrel with Snowball about Snowball's increasing popularity with the other animals. The two types of education are placed side by side for comparison: Napoleon's indoctrination of the puppies and Snowball's literacy classes.

The mystery of the disappearing milk

The mystery of the disappearing milk is explained. Can you remember how it was used in Mr Jones' time? Notice that Snowball is an accomplice in this injustice, and that he yields to the pigs' selfishness in keeping the windfall apples for their own consumption. What are Snowball's motives here? Why do you think he is taking the least difficult course of action?

Squealer to the fore

When Old Major used it, the word 'comrades' implied equality amongst the

animals. Here, Squealer uses the word to conceal the fact that they are no longer equal. While the pigs consume the milk and apples instead of sharing them out equally, Squealer is the front man who deceives and frightens the other animals. The ease with which the animals are duped over something as basic as food shows their passive acceptance of the pigs' authority.

From the start, Squealer bullies the animals into complying with the pigs' orders. Here he gives plausible excuses for the pigs' privileged position and authority. In case his 'reasons' fail to convince them, Squealer ends with the question: 'Who wants to see Jones back?' Mr Jones' tyranny is still recent enough for the animals to be persuaded that life under the pigs' authority is preferable. They are willing to submit to the pigs, so long as they keep Mr Jones away.

Self-test questions Chapters 1–3

Uncover the plot

Delete two of the three alternatives given, to find the correct plot. Beware possible misconceptions and muddles.

Mr Pilkington/Mr Jones/Mr Whymper goes to bed drunk and the animals all gather on the Knoll/in the farmhouse/in the big barn to hear Old Major/Napoleon/Boxer speak. The pig/horse/dog tells of the misery Man causes animals and preaches patience/tolerance/rebellion; finally he relates his dream of a golden future in a song: 'Animals Arise!'/'Beasts of England'/'Animal Farm'.

Old Major dies, and the animals continue to hold secret meetings, organised by the pigs/dogs/horses, the most intelligent animals. The rebellion is highly organised/planned as a military operation/spontaneous; Jones gets drunk again and forgets to feed the animals, so they drive him, his wife and his men off the farm. They bury/burn/throw away all the reins, bits, whips and knives, and enter the farmhouse with triumph/delight/fear. Napoleon/Snowball/Squealer changes the name of the farm on the gate/front door/barn wall and writes up the 5/7/10 Commandments. The corn/wheat/hay harvest is the best ever and all summer/autumn/winter the animals are happy. On Saturdays/Sundays/Mondays there is no work and their flag is hoisted – a white horn and hoof on a red/blue/green background. Snowball sums up the commandments as: 'Two/four/six legs good, two/four/six legs bad', which the cows/sheep/hens repeat endlessly. He and Napoleon/Squealer/Boxer disagree about everything. Napoleon/Squealer/Boxer takes 4/7/9 puppies away to educate them secretly. Apples and milk are reserved for the dogs/horses/pigs.

Who? What? Why? When? Where? How?

1 Who develops the concepts of Animalism?
2 Who votes on both sides on the question: Are rats comrades?
3 What do the animals do first after they have driven the humans from the farm?
4 What is the original name of Animal Farm?
5 Why does the Rebellion happen?
6 Why is the hay harvest such a success?
7 When does the Rebellion take place?
8 Where are the Seven Commandments written?
9 How does the meeting to hear Old Major speak break up?
10 How does Old Major describe Man and what does he recommend that the animals do about the human race?

Who is this?

1 Who 'seldom talked, and when he did, it was usually to make some cynical remark… Alone among the animals on the farm he never laughed.'?
2 Who 'was a brilliant talker… The others said of (him) that he could turn black into white'?
3 Who was 'always at the spot where the work was hardest'?
4 Who 'said that the education of the young was more important than anything that could be done for these who were already grown up'?
5 Who 'took a place near the front and began flirting her white mane, hoping to draw attention to the red ribbons it was plaited with'?
6 Who 'was so highly regarded on the farm that everyone was quite ready to lose an hour of sleep in order to hear what he had to say'?

7 Who was 'not much of a talker, but with a reputation for getting his own way'?

8 Who 'was a spy and a tale-bearer, but he was also a clever talker. He claimed to know of the existence of a mysterious country called Sugarcandy Mountain, to which all animals went when they died'?

9 Who 'had become much disheartened after losing money in a lawsuit, and had taken to drinking more than was good for him'?

10 Who 'was a more vivacious pig than Napoleon, quicker in speech and more inventive, but was not considered to have the same depth of character'?

A question of style

Orwell's narrative style in *Animal Farm* is direct and his language easily understood. Few words have more than three syllables and the grammatical structure is always straightforward. Orwell wrote that it was his primary aim to write: 'a story that could be easily understood by almost anyone and which could be easily translated into other languages.'

Comment on Orwell's use of language in the following quotations.

1 'Mr Jones, of the Manor Farm, had locked the hen-houses for the night, but was too drunk to remember to shut the pop-holes.' (1)

2 'All animals are equal but some animals are more equal than others.' (10)

3 'Some hams hanging in the kitchen were taken out for burial, and the barrel of beer in the scullery was stove in with a kick from Boxer's hoof, otherwise nothing in the house was touched.' (3)

4 'Napoleon had commanded that once a week there should be held something called a Spontaneous Demonstration, the object of which was to celebrate the struggles and triumphs of Animal Farm.' (9)

5 'The men fired again and again, and, when the animals got to close quarters, lashed out with their sticks and their heavy boots. A cow, three sheep, and two geese were killed, and nearly everyone was wounded. Even Napoleon, who was directing operations from the rear, had the tip of his tail chipped by a pellet.' (8)

As easy as ABC

Literacy is used by Orwell both as an indication of intelligence and of corruptibility; those animals most fluent at reading and writing are most able to use language to manipulate. Snowball, the idealist, attempts to educate the other animals and teach them the alphabet. What do we learn about the personalities and abilities of the following animals from their attempts to learn to read?

1 Mollie
2 Clover
3 Boxer
4 Benjamin
5 Muriel

Prove it!

Find a quote from the text that could be used to back up each of the following statements. (The numbers in brackets refer to the chapter you might like to look up in the commentary for help.)

1 Clover is maternal and protective (1)
2 Boxer sees hard work as the answer to every problem (3)
3 Mollie is vain (2)
4 Mollie is lazy (3)
5 Benjamin is cynical about the Rebellion (3)

Chapter 4

Napoleon and Snowball spread the news of the rebellion to animals on neighbouring farms. Mr Pilkington of Foxwood and Mr Frederick of Pinchfield, who do not get on with each other, feel threatened by the rebellion and spread rumours about Animal Farm. Mr Jones and his men try to recapture the farm, but Snowball has anticipated the attack and cleverly ambushes them. In the battle, Snowball is wounded. A stable boy is mistakenly thought to have been killed by Boxer. At the animals' victory celebration, the event is called the Battle of the Cowshed and it is decided that the victory should be celebrated annually.

Neighbours

Mr Jones is portrayed as weak and slightly ridiculous: the pub bore who cannot win the sympathy of his neighbours. His character never comes alive in the way that the main animal characters do. The human beings in the story are little more than caricatures of unpleasant types of human beings.

Revolution and corruption

Mr Pilkington of Foxwood and Mr Frederick of Pinchfield are neighbouring farmers who dislike each other as much as they dislike the deposed Mr Jones. Their behaviour is a reminder of why the revolution happened at Manor Farm. As neighbouring farmers, they have a vested interest in seeing that the revolution does not succeed but, being on bad terms with each other, they fail to join forces and overturn it. Later on, Napoleon makes use of their mutual hostility to further his own ends.

The revolution at Animal Farm makes the local farmers anxious. They act with considerable brutality to prevent similar uprisings on their own farms. But later they trade with, and then even socialise with the revolutionaries, when they realise that the pigs have become oppressors just like themselves. Notice the way the anthem 'Beasts of England' has a rallying effect when it is sung by animals on neighbouring farms. Small acts of rebellion and sabotage follow.

Even apparently trivial details reflect the precision of Orwell's political commentary. From the beginning the Russian Revolution produced opposite reactions: from the workers and journalists who saw the future in Communism to the Western Powers who considered invasion.

Battle of the Cowshed

Mr Jones attempts to recapture the farm, but once more the humans are dispatched relatively easily. The physical defeat of Mr Jones, with his men and their guns, is relatively easy for the animals. They find it far more difficult to overcome the pigs' manipulation of their emotions.

Although Mr Pilkington and Mr Frederick allow their men to help Jones in his attempt to regain his farm, they do not join in themselves. The animals do not, therefore, identify them as their enemies. What are their motives in staying behind the scenes during this battle?

Snowball's mastery of military strategy, his brilliant leadership and his personal courage during the Battle of the Cowshed are crucial to the animals' victory. However, his brilliance and success also shows Napoleon how much of a threat Snowball could be to Napoleon's own ambitions. Ironically, Snowball's military prowess here sows the seeds of his later expulsion from Animal Farm by Napoleon and his henchmen.

The Battle of the Cowshed is another amusing fusion of the animal and the human. Snowball's tactics may have come from Julius Caesar, but they are put into operation by very animal-like behaviour. See how many examples you can find of animal behaviour being deployed as part of a battle plan.

Benjamin is in the front line of attack at the Battle of the Cowshed. With Benjamin, actions always speak louder than words – unlike the pigs, who promise much but never actually deliver. Despite Benjamin's cynicism, he is the first to join in defending the farm against attack. Why doesn't he help to defend the animals against Napoleon's more sinister 'attack' on their revolutionary ideals?

The wounded Snowball demonstrates his bravery by attacking Mr Jones. But notice how easily the animals are led by propaganda to take sides against him later on – even though they witness his extreme bravery here. Squealer, like Napoleon, stays at the rear of the battle, in contrast to Snowball and Boxer.

Hero of the hour

The names of Napoleon and Squealer are conspicuous by their absence during

the battle and its aftermath. Snowball is the hero of the hour and is decorated after the battle. Remember the events of the Battle of the Cowshed as described here, and Snowball's moment of glory, because Napoleon later rewrites history to suit his own needs. This is a common practice of dictators.

Boxer and the stable boy

This incident indicates Boxer's power, already demonstrated when he destroyed the beer barrel with one kick earlier in the story. His part in the battle, particularly in knocking out the stable lad, is crucial and leads to the rout of Jones' men.

Boxer's compassion for the stable boy and his concern about what the others think about his action give insights into his character and what is important to him. His words show that he has no desire to kill anybody, merely to frighten them. Contrast Snowball's brisk, no-nonsense attitude to casualties of the battle. He has set his sights on a single goal and is not deflected by other considerations. Is this a good quality in a leader? Note the maxims that Snowball utters from time to time – for example: 'The only good human being is a dead one'. They provide an insight into the way his mind works.

The two battles

The two major conflicts – the Battles of the Cowshed and the Windmill – come at crucial moments for the animals. Led by Snowball, the animals' defence of Animal Farm is co-ordinated and united. They are proud and dignified in victory. They need no reassurance, and make their own decisions as to who should get the honours. After the Battle of the Windmill, they are depressed and weary, needing reassurance from Squealer. The victory celebrations after this battle are carefully contrived with songs, speeches and the firing of a gun – followed by the drunken debauchery of the pigs.

Chapter 5

As winter approaches, Mollie, the vain little mare, defects to the side of the humans. The animals plan the next season's work, with Napoleon and Snowball in continual disagreement. Snowball creates a plan to build a windmill which could produce enough power and energy to do much of the animals' work. He is on the point of winning the animals' vote for the project, when Napoleon signals his bodyguard of nine fierce dogs to chase Snowball off the farm. Napoleon assumes sole command, abolishes meetings and later claims the idea of the windmill as his own.

 You need detailed recall of all of *Animal Farm* (there is no padding), but perhaps Chapter 5, the end of the first half, is the most crucial turning point of all. At this point evil becomes open. A time of crisis tests the loyalty of the animals: how will Boxer, in particular, react?

A change in tone

The mood of the novel darkens in this chapter. At the beginning Orwell deals with a small-scale personal problem: Clover counselling Mollie and Mollie's desertion. This is no real loss and fits into a pattern of some animals failing to adjust to the new society. The account of Snowball planning the windmill is respectfully humorous: you can compare *One Thousand Useful Things to do about the House* with earlier examples of Snowball's studies and Orwell's comic use of incongruous names. Even Napoleon's urinating on the plans has a coarse humour to compare with the pigeons muting on the invading army. With Napoleon's call to the dogs all changes and the Terror begins.

Social change and division

Signs of social change and division are becoming apparent at Animal Farm.

The pigs now decide all questions of farm policy. At first their decisions have to be agreed by a majority vote, but later this sole remaining check on the pigs' power is discarded. A gulf has opened between Snowball and Napoleon and it becomes public during the meetings. Snowball wins popularity with 'his brilliant speeches' and clever schemes, but he fails to see the danger posed by Napoleon.

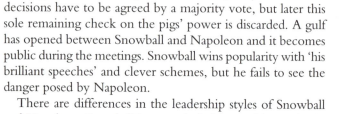

There are differences in the leadership styles of Snowball and Napoleon. Snowball has practical vision and ingenuity in educating himself and producing clever schemes to benefit everyone. He wins the hearts of the animals but fails to get their votes. Napoleon spends his time criticising Snowball's plans and making sure that the majority vote goes his way. The sheep play a crucial role in this.

The mindless responses of the sheep have a disastrous effect on the attempts of the animals to win freedom from oppression. Napoleon manipulates them to disrupt Snowball's speeches and later on to shout down all who oppose him. Their inability to think for themselves and the way they allow themselves to be manipulated at the meetings mean that the sheep play a vital part in Napoleon's rise to power.

The windmill

Snowball's plan to build a windmill to take the drudgery out of the animals' lives shows his technical ingenuity and enterprise. It gains the other animals' unstinted admiration. Napoleon's crude rejection of the plans by urinating

over them tells us more about him than anything he has said or done so far. It is a savage comment both on the nature of Napoleon's leadership and on the way that intellectuals are often treated by oppressive dictatorships.

The windmill becomes such an important and controversial issue that it divides the animals, stirring up political debate on an unprecedented and unrepeated scale. It is vital because such machinery would alter the whole structure of the farm's economic life.

Two factions

Compare the slogans of Snowball and Napoleon's supporters. Notice what Snowball visualises as the animals' society of the future. Would life have been different if Snowball had stayed in power? What evidence have we been given

Snowball

so far that Snowball is not averse to helping himself to privileges denied the other animals? Were the animals ever completely equal?

Given the pigs' greed, it is perhaps predictable that their slogan should concentrate on food. Notice its irony: whoever eats well later on, it is certainly not the working animals. Remember that much earlier in the story it was Napoleon who quickly took charge of the distribution of food after the revolution. He obviously sees the control of the food supply as crucial to maintaining power.

Problems of defence

The debate about defence finds parallels in our own society. Unfortunately,

Napoleon

because of the way in which political debate at Animal Farm has degenerated into a matter of simple opposition of whatever the other party is saying, the animals are unable to make a balanced choice between the different points of view. Snowball is keen to use propaganda to spread the revolutionary ideas, but fails to see that Napoleon uses exactly the same techniques to undermine Snowball's position with the animals. Afterwards, when he has driven Snowball from the farm, Napoleon uses the same propaganda techniques to blacken Snowball's name and to distort the animals' memory of him.

Build the windmill?

Snowball

This is a key scene. It is clear from the beginning that Napoleon has made up his mind that his power will never be secure while it can be threatened by so eloquent and persuasive a speaker as Snowball. The brevity of Napoleon's speech opposing Snowball is a foretaste of the speed and brutality of his final response.

Snowball tries to use argument and reason to persuade the animals to support the building of the windmill. He understands its potential for transforming the animals' lives. Compare Snowball's sincerity and concern for the common good with Napoleon's hypocrisy and self-interest later in the story.

Napoleon

Napoleon's quiet confidence suggests that he has planned the dogs' attack on Snowball. At this stage, could the other animals have defended Snowball and blocked Napoleon's rise to power?

Snowball's passionate appeal for the windmill triggers Napoleon's signal for the dogs' attack, emphasising the importance of the windmill as an issue. This key scene is something of a watershed. The mood of the animals' meetings changes from now on. The atmosphere becomes one of threat and fear, rather than of hope.

Snowball banished

Snowball's banishment leaves the animals at Napoleon's mercy. Do you think

Snowball

events might have been different if Snowball had been less carried away with plans and dreams, and more involved in the practicalities of running Animal Farm? Do you think it would have helped if Boxer, Benjamin and Clover had contributed more to the 'state'?

Not one of the animals had the presence of mind to ask Napoleon what he was doing with the puppies which he had taken into his care. Napoleon's gradual change into a 'human' is foreshadowed in the way the dogs obey him, just as other dogs used to obey Mr Jones.

The end of a dream?

The expulsion of Snowball marks the beginning of Napoleon's reign of terror

Revolution
and corruption

and bloodshed. The pigs now separate themselves from the other animals and take over the management of farm affairs. The atmosphere of the meetings is also different from now on. How would you describe the purpose of the Sunday meetings now and how do they differ from the earlier meetings?

The reference to the platform from which Old Major first spoke to the animals is a reminder of the way his ideals have been betrayed by Napoleon. Try to pinpoint in your mind how and why this has come about.

At the Sunday meeting, what used to be an occasion for the animals to allocate work for the week has been changed into a time when they receive their orders. The freedom to debate, and therefore to disagree, is done away with in a moment, and with it goes freedom of choice: the very thing the animals rebelled for. Saluting the flag and singing the anthem is no longer a pleasure, but a duty.

An end to protest

Some of the animals are unhappy at the turn of events but they are unable to

Communication

express their thoughts clearly. Four young porkers begin a protest but back down in the face of threats from the dogs. Napoleon later ensures that they pay the ultimate price for their opposition to him. Notice what happens to them later. The dogs' threatening growls and the sheep's mindless bleating prevent anyone from voicing further concern.

A change of status for Napoleon

None of the animals questions whether Comrade Napoleon believes all animals are equal. Nor do they object to the idea that, while they might make

mistakes, Napoleon cannot. Suddenly, Napoleon has become more than just an animal. Squealer becomes prominent in the organisation of the new society. As his spokesman, Squealer ensures that Napoleon becomes even more unapproachable and secure.

Squealer the propagandist

The crucial importance of literacy and intelligence in the fight against

oppression is shown here. Consider the skill with which Squealer subtly puts over lies, half-truths and omissions to keep the animals in docile agreement with the pigs' plans for them. If they had been less obedient and more confident of their own abilities, the other animals might have stood a chance against Squealer.

Squealer's frequent question: 'Who wants Jones back?' reinforces whatever argument he is trying to put across. This is the ultimate threat and is increasingly the only point upon which the pigs and the other animals are in agreement. Mr Jones becomes the focus of the animals' fear and, when the pigs consider it necessary, the threat of Mr Jones' return is used to unite them.

Boxer and the other animals begin to doubt their own memories and

believe Squealer's lies instead. His brain unused to thinking, Boxer decides that Napoleon's words must be true. Given the position of respect in which the other animals hold him, Boxer's maxim: 'Napoleon is always right' is disastrous. His other maxim: 'work harder', shows that he assumes hard work will solve every problem. Hard work counts for little if it is

unthinkingly applied: in many ways, Boxer oppresses himself by his refusal to use his intellect.

The windmill to be built

The announcement that the windmill is to be built after all comes as a surprise

to the animals. This is a calculated move: by announcing that the windmill is to be built, Napoleon turns the animals' attention away from the other announcements which say that during the next two years the animals must work hard for smaller rations of food. Note how frequently Napoleon uses food as a means of control and influence.

Whilst Snowball was leading the project to build the windmill, Napoleon vigorously opposed it; now that Snowball had been expelled from Animal Farm, Napoleon can support the plan. He recognises its potential value for the farm.

'The animals ... accepted his explanation'

This chapter identifies very clearly the groups which maintain Napoleon's position as dictator. The sheep are the mindless supporters, of course; the final lines show two other elements at work. The history of Snowball is already being re-written and the animals believe all, thanks to Squealer's persuasion (the propaganda machine, together with the newly-mentioned Minimus) and the threats of the dogs (secret police).

 The later stages of Chapter 5 provide fertile material for comparison to near-contemporary events (as in the essay on page 62). We see the central power base of a totalitarian dictatorship being assembled, with its fawning courtiers, arbitrary law-enforcement and distortions of truth.

Chapter 6

The second year of Animal Farm sees the animals working every day, including Sundays, on building the windmill. It takes up so much time that the harvest is less successful than the previous year's. Boxer's Herculean labour keeps the windmill project going. As some things cannot be produced by the farm, Napoleon decides to trade with the other farms. This trade is conducted through Mr Whymper, a solicitor. Squealer quells the protests of the animals. The pigs move into the farmhouse. In November a storm destroys the half-finished windmill and the absent Snowball is blamed by Napoleon.

A change for the worse

The novel can be seen as falling into two halves. Chapters 1 to 5 deal with the rebellion and a new, democratic way of life for the animals on the farm. At the beginning of Chapter 6, the animals are again living under tyrannical rule – although they reassure themselves that all is well because at least they are not working for a 'pack of idle, thieving human beings'. But who are they really working for? Chapters 6 to 10 show how their lives become harder and harder, whilst the pigs transform themselves into a 'pack of idle, thieving human beings'.

Hard work for some

Notice how the animals are punished by having their rations reduced. How much of their passivity is due to early conditioning? There is an outrageously obvious and unfair contradiction in a law which says work is strictly voluntary – but you will be punished if you don't do it. But with Boxer determined to work harder, and Benjamin presumably not prepared to comment, who is left to make a protest?

The building of the windmill involves enormous effort from the animals, especially Boxer. The animals are more or less forced to labour on it every day, and the description of breaking stones by slow and hard physical force is a reminder of the stone-breaking that convicts are traditionally forced to do when sentenced to hard labour.

Boxer in decline

Boxer's Herculean efforts to move the boulders uphill begin to tell on his physique. His strength and belief in the ideals of the revolution help him to carry out the work, but his reliance on maxims limits his understanding of what is happening to himself and to the other animals on the farm. Perhaps this combination of strength and naivety actually helps Napoleon to consolidate his dictatorship of the farm.

Boxer

Now the animals are living under a changed regime. Earlier you had the chance to assess their reactions to Jones' incompetence and cruelty and the pigs' power struggles. How do they react to a well-established dictatorship? What clearly-defined roles do Napoleon, Squealer and Boxer now fill?

Clover knows that Boxer is working too hard because his pride in his work makes him spend extra time on the windmill. Why does Boxer do this? Is he intellectually convinced of the value of the windmill or does hard labour make it easier for him to ignore what is happening around him? Perhaps he simply wishes to work harder for Animal Farm than anyone else and does not presume to question what the leadership says is needed.

Napoleon's new policy

Napoleon's 'new policy' of trading with neighbouring farms effectively breaks the animals' first commandment. Can you remember what this is? As before, an announcement about the windmill is used to distract attention from the announcement about Napoleon's trading activities involving the sale of the hens' eggs.

Napoleon

Silencing opposition

Note the growing suppression of opposition to Napoleon's authority and the mixture of threats and hollow reasoning that characterises Napoleon's dealings with the animals. The animals do not appear to notice the subtle changes which, taken together, alter the whole shape and content of the weekly meetings.

Napoleon

Squealer

Allowing no discussion, Squealer simply informs individual animals of decisions already taken. Any opposition is silenced by using the sheep's disruption at meetings and by threatening any individual who voices opposition. Consider the way in which Squealer persuades the animals to doubt their own memories. He asks them: 'have you any record of such a resolution?' The question is ironic, in view of Snowball's attempts to make the animals literate and their pitiful failure to fulfil his expectations of them.

Napoleon orders man

Note the pride the animals take in the fact that 'on all fours' Napoleon gives orders to Mr Whymper. Mr Whymper's involvement with the farm is crucial to the development of Napoleon's relationships with the neighbouring farmers. Slyness and opportunism are Mr Whymper's main qualities. Like the other human beings, his character is undeveloped, so as not to overshadow the animals. The employment of Whymper is one of several instances demonstrating the fact that Animal Farm is becoming accepted by the neighbouring farmers, though not approved. See if you can find two more examples of this acceptance of the status quo.

Utopia, for some

The rest of the animals might not have attained Utopia, but with the pigs now moving into the farmhouse and sleeping in beds, it would appear that they have achieved an ambition of sorts. Squealer's use of 'Leader' for Napoleon also adds to the distance between pigs and other animals and is part of the developing ceremonial around Napoleon. Note Squealer's insistence that because the pigs do all the 'brainwork' they deserve special privileges. Can you remember when he last used this argument, in connection with the consumption of surplus food?

Squealer

Squealer's arguments are repetitive: he feels no need to vary his style of presentation. His justification for using one of Mr Jones' beds by defining it merely as a place to sleep, ignores the luxuriousness and unnaturalness of a human bed as a place for an animal to sleep. Equally false is the distinction he draws between sheets and blankets. The animals find such arguments difficult to refute. Someone with Snowball's intelligence might have seen the gaping holes in Squealer's arguments. Snowball would have been able to see that Squealer and the other pigs are departing from the true spirit of the revolution. The phrase that clinches Squealer's argument: 'Surely none of you wishes to see Jones back?' has become familiar by now.

The value of literacy

Clover vaguely remembers some of the original revolutionary ideals and she tries to check the commandments, but she has to ask Muriel to read them to her. The changes in the commandments puzzle her but, because it is written down, she accepts it. This is the first specific amendment to the Seven Commandments, a major part of the re-writing of history. This time it occurs mysteriously; think how it later becomes obvious what is happening.

 Three of the commandments are specifically amended before the idea of equality is swept away in one single commandment. You can judge here why the animals accept the changes: Squealer's propaganda is important, but there is also lack of confidence in memory and a belief that what is written is permanent.

The windmill

The windmill gives the animals a sense of purpose and commitment. Apart from its mechanical benefits, it might also give them a sense of equality with human society. It is important, too, in developing Napoleon's status among the other farmers.

 Why is Benjamin so unenthusiastic about the windmill? Of all the animals, he comes closest to seeing the events in the story from the reader's point of view, but does his cynicism justify his refusal to act? What do you think of the way in which, having decided that the revolution will fail, he takes no part in trying to bring about its success? His defeatism renders him about as useful to the revolution as Mollie.

Benjamin

Someone to blame

The ruin of the windmill is disastrous for the animals, though in one sense helpful to Napoleon. It assists his policy of treating Snowball as an enemy of the state who can absorb blame for any failures of the leadership. What evidence is there that Snowball is guilty? What other causes are possible and which do you think the most likely?

 Like most dictators, Napoleon is unable to admit to any mistakes or errors of judgement. In Snowball, he now has someone whom he can blame for whatever goes wrong or for whatever mistakes he makes. Snowball is also used as an awful example to the rest of the animals of what happens to those who oppose Napoleon. The witch-hunt for Snowball distracts them from more serious matters.

Napoleon

Chapter 7

Bitterly cold winter weather prevents work on the windmill and there are food shortages. Mr Whymper is deceived into thinking that the food bins are full and believes Animal Farm is in a position to trade. Napoleon forces the hens to give up their eggs. There is a witch-hunt for Snowball, who is blamed for everything that goes wrong. At one point, Boxer challenges the pigs. Later, at an assembly, Napoleon has a show-trial of four of the pigs and other animals who are forced to confess to ludicrous crimes and are killed by the dogs. The dogs also attack Boxer, but he repels them. On the Knoll, Clover and the other animals try to express their grief by singing 'Beasts of England', but Squealer tells them it has been replaced by another song.

Survival

Both sides of the new animal society find inspiration in Boxer's strength: the pigs for purposes of exploitation and propaganda, the other animals for reassurance. Is this really what Old Major dreamed of for his new society? Note the tired old clichés that Squealer trots out: 'joy of service' and 'dignity of labour'.

Suddenly, the simple 'virtues' framed in the Seven Commandments take second place to the need to survive. Napoleon's deceitfulness misleads Mr Whymper so that public confidence in Animal Farm is maintained.

If the humans had discovered the animals' plight and had successfully invaded Animal Farm, would the majority of animals have been worse off? Ironically, the animals' self-sacrifice in supporting Napoleon's deception of Mr Whymper helps to keep him in power and continues the erosion of the revolution's original ideals.

Divine ruler?

Napoleon

Napoleon is becoming increasingly remote from the other animals. The ceremonial nature of his infrequent appearances at the Sunday meetings distances him from the days when he was just one of the animals. The power he assumes resembles that exercised by ancient kings and queens who ruled by 'divine right'. They believed their power to be given by God and were therefore answerable only to Him.

Squealer the intermediary

Squealer

Squealer is increasingly the only contact the animals have with the elite class of pigs, as Napoleon distances himself from the day-to-day running of the farm. Squealer, the 'propaganda machine', is the only source of contact between the animals and their ruler.

The hens' revolt

The hens' revolt is doomed to failure from the start. Note how it passes

unremarked by Boxer, Clover, Benjamin or any other of the animals. Each animal is now too self-absorbed to worry about the hens. Boxer's obsession with using his strength for only one purpose is a good example of this. The animals no longer look 'outward' to the needs of all their fellow animals, only 'inward' to what they consider important for themselves. Napoleon's success in requisitioning the hens' eggs is another defeat for the revolution's high ideals.

Trading problems

The idea of trading presupposes that there is a surplus to be traded with, which

contradicts Old Major's teaching. Is this just a case of Napoleon facing the realities of the farm's needs? How should the reader regard the sale of eggs? Perhaps Orwell is pointing out the genuine difficulties of putting ideals into practice.

What are the reasons for Napoleon's indecision about which of the two farmers he should sell his timber to? Perhaps he is aware that to do business with one of them will make trading with the other almost impossible. Perhaps he is unable to make up his mind at this point which of the two will be the most useful to him in the long term.

Napoleon steps up the witch-hunt for Snowball, using him to excuse his

Snowball

own indecision about the sale of the timber. The animals are persuaded that Snowball is responsible for the minor mishaps and petty annoyances that occur on the farm. As a result, Napoleon sets up a full investigation. This opens the way for a 'purge'. Any animal suspected of allegiance to Snowball and therefore betrayal of Napoleon, is under threat. This practice is, again, a feature of dictatorships.

Boxer asks questions

At last, Boxer questions Squealer's reinterpretation of the past. Bluntly, Boxer

Boxer

challenges Squealer and refuses to back down. Notice that when Squealer quotes Comrade Napoleon's confirmation of the story, Boxer immediately accepts the new version of events. Napoleon's position is now so far above ordinary animals that his word is taken, unquestioningly, as gospel. Boxer's disagreement has, however, been noted by Squealer who now sees him as a potential threat to the security of the pigs' power.

The importance of manipulating historical evidence, both written and remembered, is essential to Squealer's success. The only things the animals

Squealer

possess are their memory of Old Major's ideals, of events since his death, and the original Seven Commandments as written by Snowball. Squealer offers written evidence to support his condemnation of Snowball, knowing that, because of the animals' illiteracy, such 'evidence' is worthless to them. His taunt: 'if you were able to read' shows his callousness in deliberately trading on their ignorance.

Napoleon's glory

Napoleon uses medals to enhance his public image, but none of them represent any real act of bravery. Their cosmetic effect is to raise him above the rest of the animals.

Napoleon

The purge is an appalling bloodbath and finally destroys Old Major's hopes for the future. The animals' position is infinitely worse now than it was under Farmer Jones' rule, and the purge sparks revolt against the pigs.

Boxer

The dogs attack Boxer shortly after he defends Snowball's memory. There are some interesting points to note here. Boxer seems unable to grasp that Napoleon planned this attack on him. Amazingly, Boxer looks to Napoleon for orders and, at Napoleon's command, lets the dog go.

The purges and show-trials reflect events in Stalinist Russia. They also comprehensively breach the Sixth Commandment (and, by implication, several others). You should be aware of the stages by which killing animals has gone from a sin against Animalism to a commonplace.

Revolution and corruption

After the bloody and public execution of the pigs, the animals' hysteria makes them confess to 'crimes' which are mere fantasies. Show-trials in modern dictatorships provide evidence of similar public confessions, especially by those who have nothing to gain from them. The confessions have little to do with right or wrong, and everything to do with injustice and irrational, hysterical fear.

The animals, even in their numbed condition, are able to compare the purge with the way animals were slaughtered for market by Farmer Jones.

A return to the Knoll

The animals return to the Knoll, looking for comfort and reassurance, partly from Clover and partly from recalling their original hopes and ideals. Compare

Revolution and corruption

Boxer

their numb and dejected mood now with their optimism the last time they gathered at this spot.

Boxer, though shocked by the confessions and executions, misses the significance of what has happened and again falls back on his resolution to work harder. Though perhaps foolish, Boxer's conduct is also noble. Note that he never accuses Squealer of lying (he simply says, 'I do not believe that') and that his only disagreements are to defend, not to criticise, other animals. Where else can you find that approach to animal relations expressed in the book? Finally, illogically but nobly, he thinks he is partly to blame, arranges a yet earlier morning call and returns to work.

Boxer appears easy to understand, but of all the animals he perhaps poses the biggest problem in terms of assessing Orwell's attitude. How far are we to blame him for stupidity in abetting Napoleon, how far admire him for loyalty and unselfish devotion? Evidence for both can be found here.

After the purge, the animals turn to Clover for comfort. In Clover's thoughts and actions here, you can again find a strain of the idealism and devotion to the community that Boxer displays. Her memories record the changes that have taken place at Animal Farm. But Clover is unable to express her thoughts. If she had been able to do so, might she have roused the other animals to defend Old Major's vision against the corruption of the pigs?

Banned

Squealer makes light work of banning 'Beasts of England'. Revolutionary songs have the power to keep alive the flickering hopes of revolutionaries. In abolishing the anthem, Napoleon demonstrates his awareness of its potential

Squealer

danger. Minimus the poet, his very name suggesting that he has minimal talent, provides them with something else to sing – it is inferior, but safe as far as Napoleon is concerned. The new song emphasises loyalty and the animals' duty to Animal Farm: from being internationalist (trying to stir up 'beasts of every land and clime' to rebellion) it has become narrowly nationalist (promising obedience to the state).

Self-test questions Chapters 4–7

Uncover the plot

Delete two of the three alternatives given, to find the correct plot. Beware possible misconceptions and muddles.

The fame of Animal Farm grows and, in particular, its flag/song/commandments. In August/September/October, the hens/pigeons/geese bring news that Jones is leading an attack. He is defeated with only one/a few/two animal(s) killed. Snowball and Napoleon/Benjamin/Boxer are given medals for bravery. Mollie/Muriel/Clover is the first animal to desert the farm. The frequent disagreements between Snowball and Napoleon/Benjamin/Boxer reach a climax over the defence of the farm/sowing/windmill. The animals are swept away by Snowball's/Napoleon's/Squealer's eloquent pleading, but are prevented from voting for him by Napoleon's dogs who chase him away/kill him/injure him. Napoleon assumes power and abolishes Sunday meetings/the singing of 'Beasts of England'/debates. Two/three/four weeks later, he announces that the windmill will be built after all, over two/three/four years. Clover/Muriel/Boxer works the hardest in this task. Mr Frederick/Mr Whymper/Mr Pilkington is appointed to act as an intermediary in trading with humans. In September/October/November, a storm/an attack by Jones/Snowball destroys the windmill and building begins again. Food is scarce and eggs are/wheat is/wood is sold to acquire it; meanwhile Old Major/Jones/Snowball is blamed for everything that goes wrong.

Who? What? Why? When? Where? How?

1   Who first voluntarily leaves the farm and why?
2   Who invents the motto 'Napoleon is always right'?
3   Which commandment is the first to be broken?
4   What is Napoleon's answer to Snowball's plans for the windmill?
5   Why do the hens rebel?
6   Why does Napoleon ban the singing of 'Beasts of England'?
7   When do the animals fire Mr Jones' gun?
8   Where is the windmill built?
9   How is the windmill destroyed?
10 How do Napoleon and Snowball spread the word about Animal Farm?

Who is this?

1   Who 'knew that, even as things were, they were far better off than they had been in the days of Jones, and that before all else it was needful to prevent the return of the human beings'?
2   Who 'was late for work every morning and excused herself by saying that she had overslept, and she complained of mysterious pains, although her appetite was excellent'?
3   Who 'refused to believe either that food would become more plentiful or that the windmill would save work'?
4   Who 'with his books held open by a stone, and with a piece of chalk gripped between the knuckles of his trotter, (he) would move rapidly to and fro, drawing in line after line and uttering little whimpers of excitement'?
5   Who 'came creeping in under cover of darkness and performed all kinds of mischief'?

Who said that?

1   Who said: 'The only good human being is a dead one'?
2   Who said: 'do not imagine, comrades, that leadership is a pleasure! On the contrary, it is a deep and heavy responsibility.'?

3   Who said: 'The solution, as I see it, is to work harder.'?
4   Who said: 'Have you any record of such a resolution? Is it written down anywhere?'

The Seven Commandments
In this section of the novel, the first of the commandments which embody the teaching of Old Major is broken.
1   Which is it?
2   How do the pigs conceal their breach of the law?
3   How does Squealer justify it?
4   Which other commandment is broken in this section of the novel? Which are being eroded?
5   Make a list of the alterations which are made to the original commandments throughout the novel.

Prove it!
Find a quote from the text that could be used to back up each of the following statements. (The numbers in brackets refer to the chapter you might like to look up in the commentary for help.)
1   At the end of the novel, pigs and men become indistinguishable. Napoleon provides the first indication of this conclusion (5)
2   Minimus' compositions are not as uplifting as 'Beasts of England' (7)
3   Rumours about Animal Farm cause unrest throughout the animal kingdom (4)
4   Not all the pigs agree with Napoleon's rules (5 and 6)

Chapter 8

The Sixth Commandment is altered to provide an excuse for the killings. Napoleon remains aloof from the animals, a remote leader-figure. Squealer regularly gives glowing reports of the farm's progress. Napoleon plays Pilkington and Frederick off against each other over the proposed sale of timber. Frederick buys the timber with counterfeit bank notes. He then attacks Animal Farm and blows up the windmill. This enrages the animals, who drive off the humans, but at great cost. Boxer is wounded in what comes to be known as the Battle of the Windmill. After subdued victory celebrations, the pigs get drunk on Farmer Jones' whisky.

The Sixth Commandment: 'No animal shall kill any other animal'

Why should Benjamin refuse to 'meddle' when Clover asks him to read the Sixth Commandment? To read them has not yet been declared a crime. It is, however, significant that the animals are now too frightened to read.

Muriel again helps Clover by reading the Sixth Commandment to her. As

always, Clover can remember more clearly than the others, but not quite clearly enough. The general inability to read and write has ensured that there has never been more than one copy of the commandments, so there is nothing to verify what they originally said. Remember the tremendous

Communication importance which Snowball attached to literacy. Do you believe the 'lists of figures' Squealer reads from some paper? None of the animals is in a position to contradict him.

Absolute authority

Note how Napoleon distances himself from the other animals, even the pigs.

Napoleon

The image he projects when he does appear makes him seem larger than life. He has used Animalism and the revolution to feed his ego and has instituted a regime which will serve his every wish. His authority is now absolute.

The fawning poem 'Comrade Napoleon' is of poor literary quality, cliché-ridden and full of meaningless nationalism and pretentions. The poem is a parody of the sort of dreadful official verse tyrannical dictatorships such as Stalinist Russia encourage. It is so exaggerated as to become comic. See how many ridiculous features of style you can find. One excellent form of mockery is the series of absurd rhymes for 'Napoleon': 'soul is on', etc.

Ritual slaughter

Can you think of anything more unlikely than that three small hens should

Revolution and corruption

plot to kill a pig of Napoleon's size? In fact, the hens' 'conspiracy' is simply an excuse for the pigs to carry out a ritual slaughter. Its purpose is to provide a public demonstration of their power to keep the other animals in fear and terror. It is intended to deter animals who might be contemplating revolution. The death of a few hens out of so many will not have any adverse affect on egg production and is not so controversial as the deaths of Boxer or Clover might have been. It is typical of such a society that the weakest are the most oppressed.

A sale agreed

Napoleon's public declaration that he is to sell timber to Pilkington is

Communication

accompanied by a series of rumours about Frederick's cruelty to his animals. These rumours are similar to those about Animal Farm which were spread in its early days. The details sound like a product of Squealer's propaganda machine. The rumours are put about to provide 'justification' for Napoleon's decision to deal with Pilkington rather than with Frederick.

As yet the reader has not met Frederick and Pilkington face to face. Most of what we know of them is hearsay.

Squealer

Note Squealer's sinister role in the post-revolution society – emphasised here by the 'suicide' of the gander. The 'suicides' of political activists form another feature of oppressive regimes. Note that there are few creative activities in the animals' lives now. Apart from work, the only social events at the farm are the continued blackening of Snowball's character, death-threat slogans directed against Frederick and news of plots and suicide. Compare this to the hive of creative activity which Snowball encouraged. The animals' social and cultural environment is dreary indeed.

The windmill is finished

The completion of the windmill is a triumph for the animals, but it presents something of a problem for Napoleon. Until now he has been able to keep the animals occupied with this tremendous enterprise. Now that it is finished, will the animals use their leisure to brood about the injustices in their present lives, and to consider whether their existence has improved since they overthrew Farmer Jones? Napoleon identifies himself with the success of the windmill by appearing at the ceremony in order to name it 'Napoleon Mill'.

You need to think about the importance of names in *Animal Farm*; e.g. the farm itself changes name twice, Old Major is known to men as Willingdon Beauty, 'our Leader, Comrade Napoleon' (a contradiction in itself) has scores of titles, plus a mill named after him. Why are names so important politically?

A suspect deal

Frederick removes the timber from Animal Farm with almost indecent haste. Do you find this suspicious? In Frederick, Napoleon seems to have met his equal in ruthlessness. Perhaps Napoleon has made the mistake of thinking that he is dealing with illiterate, bemused animals rather than with a fellow 'dictator'.

Another attack on Animal Farm

In an endeavour to salvage prestige amongst the animals, Napoleon pronounces the death sentence on Frederick. How serious do you think this is? The stationing of sentries and the message to Pilkington sharpen the animals' awareness of the need to prepare for war.

The bargaining with Pilkington and Frederick, coupled with a propaganda war against whoever is out of favour, echoes Stalin's dealings with Hitler's Germany and the West in the late 1930s. You will recognise the sort of rumours spread about Frederick's treatment of the workers as being applicable to Nazi Germany. Napoleon's deal with Frederick matches Stalin's pact with Hitler, which was also followed by betrayal and invasion. Just as in *Animal Farm*, the German invasion brought great destruction of the industrial base, a heroic defence and the retreat of the invaders.

This section is a good example of George Orwell's ability to run an animal story and a powerful satire simultaneously. Thanks to characters like Boxer and Clover, we sympathise with the animals, even while despising much of the behaviour of the leadership and appreciating the precise connections to events of 1939–41.

The Battle of the Windmill

During the Battle of the Windmill, Napoleon seems unable to cope for the

Boxer

first time. The superior weapons used by the humans easily repel the animals.

This time Boxer and Napoleon come together in the defence of the farm, as Boxer and Snowball did in the Battle of the Cowshed. Boxer never fully appreciates his own worth or his potential to become a good influence. This lack of self-confidence is Boxer's greatest fault.

The destruction of the windmill by Frederick justifies Napoleon's warnings to the animals about the threat posed by humans. It helps us to understand why they continue to tolerate Napoleon's domination.

Destruction of the windmill

The Battle of the Windmill unites the animals in one last effort. Look back

Revolution and corruption

to the previous attempts to invade Animal Farm and compare the animals' motives then with their anger now. The mood of this battle is quite different, with its 'savage, bitter' fighting resulting in a high casualty rate. Despite his courage when the windmill is blown up, Napoleon is soon back in his accustomed place, directing operations from the rear while the battle is being fought. Compare his wounds (his tail is 'chipped by a pellet') with those Snowball sustained at the Battle of the Cowshed.

After the battle

Squealer

Squealer's actions again contradict his words. Although absent from the battle, he claims it a glorious victory for the long-suffering animals. However, Boxer's memory of the battle is still fresh, and he challenges Squealer. For the first time, Boxer appears to be thinking about the implications of what has happened.

Communication

Notice the ambiguity in Squealer's speech; 'victory' is really open to several interpretations. What he says is strictly correct, but who has really gained or lost the battle? Words like 'justice', 'terrorist/freedom fighter' and 'freedom' can also mean different things, depending on an individual's point of view or position in a particular society.

Notice how the unification of the animals is engineered and how symbols of victory and patriotism are used to manipulate their emotions. Napoleon has become such a symbol, and here he creates another, the 'Order of the Green Banner'.

However, despite the manipulation of emotions via propaganda and symbols, you should note that the heroism and sense of unity displayed by the ordinary farm animals are genuine. If you look at the beginning of the last chapter of Animal Farm, you will find a pride in the farm undimmed by the passing of time and the pigs' exploitation of the other animals.

A new Napoleon?

The post-battle propaganda by Napoleon and the whisky celebration by the pigs, which excludes the working animals, show the division between the leaders and the led. Alcohol caused the animals to suffer in the past. Has this really been a 'victory' of the pigs over the animals?

Napoleon

Does the drunken Napoleon reveal his true ambition by wearing Farmer Jones' bowler hat? Typical of his now-bankrupt leadership is Napoleon's 'illness', obviously a severe hangover, and the resultant decree that drinking alcohol is punishable by death. This decree is soon annulled when it is announced that Napoleon has ordered brewing equipment. Animal Farm is now being run for the convenience of the pigs. Even Napoleon's hangover is blamed on Snowball.

The pigs' contempt for the animals' welfare is further shown when Napoleon uses the intended retirement grazing ground to grow barley from which whisky can be made. In view of the animals' desperate situation, this is a particularly ironic example of the discrepancy between what is considered essential for rulers and what is thought suitable for those they rule.

New commandments

Revolution and corruption

When Squealer used to hold the paint pot for Snowball and stood behind him on the ladder, he had slightly more success than he has on this occasion. How many of the Commandments have now been altered? Can you remember when the alterations were discovered? Look at the detailed description of what the animals see when they investigate the cause of the loud crash. Yet none of them can 'form any idea' of its cause. With the evidence of Squealer's activities so plain, their reaction is almost unbelievable. It shows the degree to which they are now unable to think for themselves. Only Benjamin still has the presence of mind to realise what is going on.

Muriel's unquestioning acceptance of the new Fifth Commandment highlights the fact that the animals no longer trust their own memories.

Chapter 9

Boxer begins to age, but continues to labour at the rebuilding of the windmill. Rations are reduced, except for those of the pigs and dogs. Thirty-one pigs are born, and their privileged education is supervised by Napoleon. Compulsory 'spontaneous demonstrations' are held. Squealer provides figures to show how much 'better' life is now than it was in Farmer Jones' day. Moses the raven returns and tells the animals about Sugarcandy Mountain. Animal Farm is declared a republic, with one candidate for President: Napoleon. Boxer collapses and is taken off to the slaughterhouse. Squealer claims Boxer died in hospital, but Benjamin knows better. There is a grotesque memorial banquet, attended only by the pigs.

Various concerns

Despite their callous treatment by the pigs, the animals still have real concern

Boxer

for each other. Boxer's unselfishness and pride in his work again cause concern to his lifelong companions, Clover and Benjamin. Again, Boxer dreams of the completion of the windmill and the fulfilment of a promised retirement. Why do you think he is unable to see that, after years of frustrated promises, such dreams are unlikely to be fulfilled?

Clover realises that Boxer needs to rest, but she is unable to help him properly. She is concerned in a straightforward and practical way. Compare her sympathy and 'poultice of herbs' with the pigs' indifference and Napoleon's 'pink medicine' later on.

Confused memories

Revolution and corruption

The use of Jones's return as a threat is still effective in subduing the animals, as is the comparison between post-revolution life and the bad old days under Farmer Jones. By now the animals are too confused to trust their own memories, after submitting to so much propaganda and so many distortions of the truth.

Improved status and conditions – for some

The young pigs are kept apart from the other animals and are trained to become the new elite. Note how the privileges and status which the pigs now enjoy create a 'superior' class within the animals' society.

Napoleon

By now, Napoleon's standard of living far exceeds that enjoyed by Farmer Jones. In some respects, Old Major was right when he said the animals could manage the farm better than Man. But he failed to allow for the worst side of the pigs' character coming into play so strongly or for the different levels of ambition and ability among the various animals.

Notice how wistfully the animals long for better treatment from the pigs. Notice too how brutally indifferent the pigs are to the needs and emotions of the working animals. Compare this with Jones' careless kindness in putting surplus milk in the hens' mash.

Propaganda and Ceremonial

Though this chapter contains one of the most moving incidents of the novel,

Squealer

the death of Boxer, much of it consists of descriptions of what life is like now that a certain stability has come to Animal Farm and dictatorship remains unchallenged. Squealer's propaganda reaches new heights, with his 'readjustment' of rations and documentary proof that the animals are not short of food. See what other examples of propaganda you can find and note how absurdly far from reality Snowball's reputation has now moved. What do you think the reaction would have been a few years earlier if Squealer had said that he had fought openly on Jones' side and been wounded by Napoleon?

Hand in hand with propaganda goes ceremonial. Again you can find several examples, but the most striking is probably the compulsory Spontaneous Demonstration which echoes all those dramatic military parades in Red Square, Moscow.

Moses the raven

Moses returns to Animal Farm and tells the animals of the delights of Sugarcandy Mountain. Moses represents, to some extent, Orwell's view of the more corrupt aspects of organised religion. Why do the pigs seem to welcome Moses' return and the unsettling effect he has on the animals? Note the similarities between Farmer Jones' attitude to Moses and that of the pigs. They treat him as a pet, just as Mr Jones did. The pigs are quite happy for the animals to spend their time striving for a better afterlife, so long as it doesn't affect their work here and now. In addition, they perhaps welcome the distraction that Moses provides, as it helps the animals to forget their empty bellies.

Boxer's declining years

Boxer

Benjamin

Boxer's physical decline comes at a time when the pigs' power is virtually unchallenged and the revolutionary ideals, at least for the majority of the animals, long-forgotten. All that Boxer can look forward to is his retirement.

Squealer's response to Boxer's illness gives the animals a moment of concern. But Squealer has little difficulty in reassuring them. Benjamin demonstrates his love for Boxer by staying with him and keeping the flies away. No doubt he feels he is being very helpful, but would he have been of more help if he had used his brains to try and warn the animals, particularly Boxer, about the pigs' erosion of their revolutionary ideals?

Napoleon

Napoleon shows his callousness and his indifference to suffering in his premeditated disposal of Boxer. Even for the sake of a public relations exercise he cannot bring himself to visit Boxer, merely ordering a bottle of pink medicine from Jones' medicine chest to be sent over – medicine that is of little use to Boxer.

Spurred to action – too late

Benjamin

Benjamin pushes Muriel aside and reads the clearly written message out to the assembled animals. For so long inactive, when he does stir himself to action, it is too late. Clover races after the van and calls Boxer to try and escape – but in vain.

The death of Boxer is full of ironies: the fact that Benjamin finally acts decisively and displays passion and anguish, only to be ignored until it is too late, is only one of them. There is the fact that Boxer is taken to his death by his own kind who are too 'stupid' and 'ignorant' to respond, but who could be seen as doing their duty. How do you think Boxer would have responded in the same situation? Finally, of course, there is the irony that Boxer's strength has been spent in the service of Animal Farm and now he lacks the power to break out of the van.

Boxer's end

Boxer

Boxer was first described as having a 'somewhat stupid appearance'. In the light of what has happened, what is your opinion of Boxer's character? The knackers' van which takes Boxer is horribly reminiscent of the mobile extermination vans used by Hitler to transport Jews to the concentration camps.

The death of Boxer finally confirms that loyalty in dictatorships is a one-way process. It is a good example of an incident that makes more general comment on the horrors of 1930s Europe. People who thought it could not happen to them were not confined to Russia: think of Jews who never believed what Nazism could lead to.

Squealer

In the speech he makes after Boxer has been taken away, Squealer is at his most hypocritical, callous and cunning. Quickly glossing over Boxer's death, he merely uses it as an excuse for a hymn in praise of Napoleon.

Napoleon takes care to associate himself with the grief felt by the animals at Boxer's death and he expediently reminds them of Boxer's two maxims. As always, Napoleon turns the occasion to his own advantage.

The final ironies are part of the lies of the propaganda machine. Only the pigs derive benefit from Boxer's death which they have organised, but they manage hypocritical tributes to his memory. Worst of all, Napoleon excuses the fact that they cannot bury his body on the farm by speaking of the memorial banquet which will honour Boxer. The result: more whisky, paid for by selling the remains of the subject of the memorial banquet.

Chapter 10

Several years have passed; some animals have died, but none have retired, even though the farm prospers. No one can remember life before the revolution and they take pride in their unique society. Suddenly the pigs appear, standing upright on two legs and carrying whips. The sheep have a new slogan and the Seven Commandments have been reduced to one. The pigs have adopted a human lifestyle. The final scene shows pigs and men together at a party. Napoleon announces that the farm will revert to its original name, Manor Farm. The onlooking animals look from pig to man and back again and realise that they look exactly alike.

A working windmill

The windmill is at last complete. Look back to Snowball's vision of the benefits it would bring the animals and compare it with the reality. What good has the windmill done the animals who laboured so long to build it? What good is it doing them now? Who really benefits from the windmill's creation of energy?

Beasts of England

Revolution
and corruption

The animals cling to Old Major's vision and 'Beasts of England' is sung in secret. Perhaps the revolution is coming full circle? Squealer takes the sheep away to learn a new song, a preparation for the pigs' abandonment of animal status: a reminder, perhaps, of Napoleon removing the puppies to 'educate' them?

A new disguise for Napoleon

Do you think that Clover's terrified neighing suggests that she has awoken to

Napoleon

what happens around her? Or is it simply a response to the fact that she can no longer distinguish between pig and man? The appearance of Napoleon, walking on two legs and carrying a whip in his trotter, openly shows the true nature of his power.

Napoleon has achieved what he most envied in man – to be able to walk on two legs. Once again, the animals' protest is drowned by the sheep's carefully rehearsed chanting. Traditionally viewed as stupid and easily led, the sheep are used by the pigs as a tool of government.

'Some animals are more equal than others'

Benjamin

Ironically, the first time Benjamin is persuaded to read aloud, he reads the death-knell of the animals' revolutionary ideals. He, of all the animals, is the most likely to understand the implications of what the remaining commandment says, yet he makes no comment. Why?

George Orwell understood well the importance of slogans in politics, particularly in totalitarian politics. *Animal Farm* contains many memorable slogans, several of which occur in this last chapter. Now that 'Four legs good, two legs better' and 'some animals are more equal than others' have changed the social climate, see how many examples you can find of details, some quite homely, which show the pigs' transformation into equivalents of mankind.

A new uniform for Napoleon

Napoleon now wears Farmer Jones' clothes: he has succeeded in replacing him in every respect. This foreshadows the final scene of the novel, when

Napoleon

Revolution
and corruption

Napoleon is indistinguishable from his insolent human guests.

There is a certain irony in the way Pilkington congratulates the pigs, not on the efficiency of the farm but in the fact that the animals on Animal Farm do more work for less food than the animals on any other farm. In other words, he congratulates the pigs on their ability to exploit the animals.

Having received Pilkington's praise for the wretched conditions endured by the animals, Napoleon removes the last of the revolution's effects: the animals are no longer to address each other as 'Comrade'; the parades to honour Old Major are to be abandoned (his skull has already been buried); the flag is to be changed to a plain green – what used it to show? The signs are that the future for the animals will be far worse than anything they knew under Farmer Jones. Things come full circle with the renaming of the farm, Manor Farm.

The Tehran conference in 1943 (according to Orwell, the original of this scene) was between Stalin and the leaders of the Allies against Hitler, so where does that place Frederick (i.e. Germany) in the celebration at the farmhouse? Check any references to Frederick in the last three chapters. You should also note that the book ends in disagreement: this is the route Orwell rightly anticipated relations between the West and the USSR would take.

The ending of *Animal Farm* is perfectly judged. It is the proof of 'more equal than others'; it provides a telling visual image (animals looking in as outsiders at the grotesque party); it completes a narrative circle with the re-naming, etc: it is also totally up-to-date (1943) in its final political comment.

Pigs or men?

The final vision, presented through Clover's dim old eyes, is of pigs and men becoming indistinguishable. Does Clover understand the betrayal that has taken place?

Revolution and corruption

The cycle of corruption is complete. For the animals, it seems there is little to choose between one master and another. The story ends as it began, with the masters of Animal Farm drinking too much, but this time the animals hear no optimistic dream of a new future with a just society. All power corrupts, and absolute power corrupts absolutely, but how and why did it happen at Animal Farm? How far were the animals responsible? Are there any lessons for us as individuals or for our society to learn from *Animal Farm*?

■ Self-test questions Chapters 8–10

Uncover the plot

Delete two of the three alternatives given to find the correct plot. Beware possible misconceptions and muddles.

Napoleon continues to become less tyrannical/accessible/reasonable; he plays Pilkington/Whymper/Jones and Frederick against each other over the proposed sale of eggs/land/timber, and is disappointed/hysterical/enraged when he discovers he has been tricked. Frederick/Pilkington/Jones attacks the farm and destroys the windmill with gunpowder/sledgehammers/bulldozers. Six animals are killed but the humans are defeated. To celebrate, the pigs drink rum/gin/whisky. Boxer/Benjamin/Napoleon has injured his leg/hoof/back but is due to retire on this 10th/11th/12th birthday. Rations are reduced/adjusted/increased and Animal Farm becomes a monarchy/Republic/Democracy. Benjamin/Clover/Boxer collapses and is sold to the slaughterhouse by the pigs/humans/other horses, who hold a memorial service/banquet/meeting in his honour. Weeks/months/years pass and the farm grows richer/poorer/smaller. Many/few/none of the animals remember life before the rebellion and they still have pride/joy/comfort in their farm; this is destroyed when the pigs begin to wear clothes/stand upright/walk on their hind legs. Only one/two/three of the commandments remain(s) and in the final scene, pigs and humans are shown in a serious meeting/at a party/at a dance. Animal Farm is now to be called Napoleon Farm/Windmill Farm/Manor Farm. When the pigs and men start to agree/argue/drink together, they become indistinguishable from each other.

Who? What? Why? When? Where? How?

1 Who attends Napoleon when he appears in public?
2 Who starts the argument between men and pigs, and why?
3 What does Napoleon, walking on his hind legs, carry?
4 What do the pigs buy with the money they earn by selling Boxer to the knacker's yard?
5 Why do you think that Napoleon is the only animal not to fall on his belly and hide his face when the windmill is blown up?

6 Why do the animals peer in through the window to observe the pigs and the humans?
7 When is Animal Farm declared a Republic?
8 Where does the meeting between pigs and men take place?
9 How many times do the animals rebuild the windmill?
10 How many men take part in the Battle of the Windmill?

Who is this?
1 Who 'was about to spring some carefully prepared witticism on the company, but for a moment he was too overcome by amusement to be able to utter it'?
2 Who 'had bought himself a dogcart'?
3 Who 'made his appearance, walking slowly and dejectedly, his eyes dull, his tail hanging limply behind him, and with every appearance of being seriously ill'?
4 Who 'proved to them in detail that they had more oats, more hay, more turnips than they had had in Jones' day'?
5 Who 'temporarily stunned, was sprawling beside it, and near at hand there lay a lantern, a paintbrush, and an overturned pot of white paint'?
6 Who 'was much the same as ever, except for being a little greyer around the muzzle, and, since Boxer's death, more morose and taciturn than ever'?

Who writes?
1 Who writes: 'Serves you right.'?
2 Who writes: 'All animals are equal but some are more equal than others'?
3 Who writes: 'Friend of the fatherless
                 Fountain of happiness!
                 Lord of the swill-bucket!'?
4 Who writes: '...mysterious things called "files", "reports", "minutes" and "memoranda" '?

Taking sides
Orwell's animal community – in common with most, if not all human communities – mixes basically good characters and villains with the ordinary mass of population.
1 Divide the named animals into 'good' and 'bad' characters.
2 Which groups of animals represent the general mass of common people?
3 Which animals survive at the end of the novel?
4 Which single (nameless) animal falls outside the categorisation of 'good' and 'bad'?

Prove it!
Find a quote from the text that could be used to back up each of the following statements. (The numbers in brackets refer to the chapter you might like to look up in the commentary for help.)
1 Benjamin loves Boxer (9)
2 Clover loves Boxer (9)
3 Moses the raven is useful to the pigs (9)
4 Napoleon is paranoid (like many dictators) about being attacked or poisoned (8)
5 The sheep, however stupid, are capable of learning new tricks (10)

How to write an examination essay

Most of you will be studying *Animal Farm* as a set text for your formal examination. This section gives you some guidelines on how to approach an examination essay and also considers three possible subjects.

Before you start writing

The first essential is thorough revision. It is important that you realise that even Open Book examinations require close textual knowledge. You will have time to look up quotations and references, but *only if you know where to look*.

- Read the questions very carefully, both to choose the best one and to take note of *exactly* what you are asked to do. Do not answer the question you imagine or hope has been set, or repeat the practice essay you wrote earlier on a similar but *slightly different* subject.

- Identify all the key words in the question that mention characters, events and themes, and instructions as to what to do, e.g. compare, contrast, comment, explore, explain, etc. It is very unlikely that simple retelling of the story will gain you much credit.

- Look at the list of points you have identified and jot down what you are going to write about each.

- Decide in what order you are going to deal with the main points. Number them in sequence. This is a matter of choice, but do not use chronological order unless you have a good reason to.

Writing the essay

- The first sentences are important. Try to summarise your response to the question so the examiner has some idea of how you plan to approach it. Do not begin, 'Snowball fought bravely at the Battle of the Cowshed and was wounded. He also tried hard to educate the animals.' A good beginning to an essay on the characters of the pigs might be, 'From the outset Napoleon and Snowball are presented as rivals, in constant disagreement. Though Snowball is both more imaginative and more devoted to the welfare of the animals, Napoleon's triumph is gained through ruthlessness and the methods of a totalitarian state.' Jump straight into your argument; do not waste time at the start. A personal response is rewarded, but you must always answer the question – as you write your essay, *refer back to your list of points*.

- Answer *all of the question*. Many students spend all their time answering just one part of a question and ignoring the rest. This prevents you gaining marks for the parts left out. In the same way, failing to answer enough questions on the examination is a waste of marks which can always be gained most easily at the start of an answer.

- There is no 'correct' length for an essay. What you must do is to spend the full time usefully in answering all parts of the question (spending longer than the allocated time by more than a few minutes is dangerous). Some people write faster than others, but they don't always get the best marks!

- Take care with presentation, spelling and punctuation. It is generally unwise to use slang or contractions (e.g. 'they've' for 'they have').

- Use quotation or paraphrase when it is relevant and contributes to the quality and clarity of your answer. References to events often do not need quotation, but the exact words of for instance, the Seven Commandments (original and amended), Squealer's propaganda speeches or the sheep's chants are valuable.

Example questions

Below are three examples of the kind of questions you may expect in your exam. An *outline* of a model answer has been supplied for each question. You will find it useful to write full-length versions of these plans, incorporating references from the text to back up the ideas.

1 Animal Farm *was first published in 1945 at the end of the Second World War. Orwell called it 'A Fairy Story'.*
   What do you think the book has to say both about the time at which it was written and about other times in history? (NEAB specimen question)

- Much useful material for this will be found in the introductory section on **George Orwell, satire and the Russian Revolution**, as well as in the **Text commentary**. The arranging of the material is, however, crucial. You need to make a connection between the first half of the question and the second. Why does it mention 'Fairy Story'? This surely is inviting you to prove that in reality it is much less harmless than that, so you should consider what type of a story it is, with particular emphasis on its purpose as satire.

- There is also something slightly misleading in the question. The first half gives the date 1945, the second half refers to 'the time at which it was written' which was 1943–44, a very different time when the war was not yet won. You could point out that the attack on Russian Communism was particularly daring at the time the book was written. (The background information for this is in the **George Orwell, satire and the Russian Revolution** section.)

- There are three main sections of your essay, the first two relating to Orwell's own time and the third relating to 'other times in history'. First you need to explain how the novel satirises the Russian Revolution and the Soviet Union under Stalin. Explain how up-to-date the novel is, ending with the 1943 Tehran Conference. Beware of becoming bogged down in every little detailed comparison, but explain the main connections of people and events.

- Secondly, turn to the twentieth century in general and George Orwell's ideals of freedom of speech and action, democracy and clarity and honesty of communication. Explain how examples of torture of minorities, totalitarian states, purges of dissidents, censorship and propaganda were all around him. Britain was fighting a war against Fascism in Germany and Italy, Orwell himself had earlier fought against Fascism in Spain. In *Animal Farm* he attacks the USSR specifically and dictatorships in general.

- In other times in history dictatorships have frequently developed from revolutions preaching equality: a good example is the Emperor Napoleon (that name again!) who rose to power via the French Revolution. You will need to examine the way in which human (or in this case porcine) ambition takes over from idealism and a new elite is created: not by any means unique to the Russian Revolution. Examine the different types who so often play a part in revolutions: from the idealists to the power-seekers, from the propagandists to the deceived populace.

- There are many ways to end the essay. A neat final paragraph would bring us round in a circle, explaining that the strength of *Animal Farm* lies partly in its convincing blend of the general (human nature in times of revolution) and the specific (the story of Stalin, Trotsky and the rest).

2 *Compare and contrast the ways in which **two** of the following characters deal with their situation on the farm:*

>   *Napoleon*
>   *Snowball*
>   *Boxer*
>   *Mollie*
>   *Squealer*

You should consider:
>   *their motives*
>   *their methods of trying to achieve what they want*
>   *what Orwell wants you to think about them.*

(NEAB specimen question)

- There is no shortage of material here and a question like this does much of your organising for you. You need to be particularly careful to do everything you are told to do. You must write on six things: three aspects of two animals. You must also *compare and contrast*: find the similarities and differences.

- The first decision is the choice of animals. Napoleon would be a good choice because there is a vast choice of material and Orwell makes it clear what view he takes of him. Beware of choosing a character that appears almost too easy: do you really have enough to say about Mollie? Any of the others would be suitable. Let us assume that you are writing about Napoleon and Squealer.

- The next decision is whether to deal with motives, methods, etc, taking in both Napoleon and Squealer, or to devote the first half to Napoleon, the second to Squealer. Either is suitable, but, if you choose the second, you must remember to keep up the comparison: 'Unlike Napoleon, Squealer does not seek power for himself' or, 'Squealer possesses the powers of oratory that Napoleon lacks.'

- Let us assume that you choose to consider each of the three areas with both pigs. Motives for Napoleon are straightforward enough: ambition, greed, lust for power, etc. Finding proof is essential, but not difficult. Squealer's motivation is a little less obvious. He is not a boar, merely a porker, and is not going to achieve eminence as a leader himself. Attaching himself to a leader gives him a kind of surrogate power and also the comfort he so obviously desires: by the last chapter he is very well fed indeed!

- In the method section your two subjects intertwine. Napoleon's methods are based on doing what he knows he can do and employing others to do what he cannot. A dominating presence and qualities of determination, single-mindedness and ruthlessness serve him well, and he trains up loyal minions like Minimus, the dogs and the cockerel. Foremost among these is Squealer: you should enjoy explaining his methods, based upon lies, twisted statistics, recurrent catch-phrases and an engaging manner: copious quotation required!

- It is clear what Orwell wants us to think about Napoleon and Squealer: in different ways both are despicable. How are you going to prove it? You might like to bring up the total absence of honesty (detailed examples, please), the way they treat honourable characters like Snowball or Boxer and a cross-reference to their human equivalents.

- There is no obvious conclusion to a necessarily divided essay. A straight-forward summary would be adequate, but for a change why not consider which of the two is more worthy of the contempt and distaste of the reader? There is no right answer: make up your own mind and present a case, using examples of events and Orwell's descriptions and comments.

3 In *Chapter 2 there were Seven Commandments. By Chapter 10 there is only one Commandment: ALL ANIMALS ARE EQUAL, BUT SOME ANIMALS ARE MORE EQUAL THAN OTHERS. Describe and explain how and why the Seven Commandments were replaced by one.* (NEAB specimen question)

- Though this question is not difficult, you must beware of the danger of narration. Telling the story of all the changes in the Commandments is not enough, though you should refer to every one of those changes. You are asked to explain as well as describe and also to consider the how and why.

- At some stage (and the beginning is probably the best place to do this) you have to explain in some detail how the Seven Commandments are simply a reflection of the state of the farm and the beliefs of the animals. The Seven Commandments are an attempt to codify a set of ideals, and belong to the time when idealism and comradeship fuelled the animals' actions. The single Commandment is the expression of an elitist dictatorship of the pigs. Therefore the background answer to 'Why?' comes in the overall changes on the farm, the collapse of idealism and the revolutionary spirit.

- You then need to explain what happened to each commandment individually. You will find an individual reason for the removal of each in the pigs' self-interest. Some of these are general, the first two and the seventh, for instance: the pigs no longer see all animals as friends and equals and all humans as enemies. Some are more specific: once the pigs have discovered a taste for whisky and beer, Number 5 must go.

- The response to 'How?' comes in two separate categories. Some are specifically amended, always after the event: the executions lead to 'No animal shall kill any other animal *without cause*.' Others are simply ignored until finally 'justified' by the last amendment which excuses all the pigs' excesses.

- In a sense the answer to 'How?' is in some cases as simple as, 'Squealer climbed up with a pot of paint and altered the commandment.' However, you should look at the broader 'How?': 'How did they manage to get away with destroying the basic rules of the Rebellion?' Short memories, big dogs and effective propaganda are three reasons; you may well think of others.

- It is possible to write a reasonable essay by charting the change in the Commandments one by one. However, relating all this to the central theme of the book makes a much better essay. Why not finish by emphasising that the whole tragedy of *Animal Farm* is summed up in the destruction of the Seven Commandments?

■ How to write a coursework essay

Most of you are unlikely to have to write a coursework essay on *Animal Farm*, but you may wish to use the book as the twentieth-century comparison to pre-twentieth century fiction in a Wide Reading assignment. If you do so, you should bear in mind the following points:

- There must be a *specific* ground for comparison. The comparison should be made throughout the essay, not necessarily in the same sentence, but at least in adjacent paragraphs.

- You can use *Animal Farm* with a very different novel or story, but there must be one definite respect (or more than one) in which you can find similarities or differences or both.

- You do not need to look for books about farms or animals. However, finding suitable uses for *Animal Farm* as a comparison is not especially easy. Dickens is a possibility. You could look into his attacks on the heartlessness of mankind (a choice of many novels), but the most interesting comparison in Dickens would be the presentation of revolution in *A Tale of Two Cities* and *Animal Farm*. Both discover the cruelty and selfishness beneath apparent idealistic fervour, though Dickens' viewpoint is more reactionary and his methods totally different. Dickens attacks the abuses of revolution mainly through the creation of sympathetic characters and a strong story-line that blends action, romance and pathos.

- However, there is one author for whom *Animal Farm* makes a perfect comparison: Jonathan Swift. Both Swift and Orwell use a clear and elegant style and apparently detached manner to express their disgust at the absurd cruelties of mankind. Swift's short satire, *A Modest Proposal*, maintains a dead-pan style while advocating the slaughter and consumption of children in apparent seriousness. The surface coolness can be compared to Orwell's 'fairy story'. If you were to write on *Gulliver's Travels*, you would even find a final section presenting horses as equivalents to Man, though they are much more intelligent than Boxer!

- There are possible political novels by such authors as Anthony Trollope, but these are very different in tone and method: the most effective use of *Animal Farm* is likely to be as a comparison to Swift.

With any coursework essay (whether a comparison or a study of one text) there are certain considerations always to be borne in mind:

- It is essential that you show considerable evidence of textual knowledge, even if the essay has a strong creative element.

- In an analytical essay the most important consideration is that you must develop an argument or explain a point of view throughout. Careful advance preparation will aid you in organising your theme or argument: making notes on the material, putting these notes in order, then working through two or three drafts of the essay. In this way you should be able to make a decision on what each paragraph is about, as far as possible signalling that to the reader in the opening sentence, often called a *topic sentence* because it states the topic of the paragraph.

- If you are writing an imaginative/creative essay, the first essential is to reveal throughout your factual knowledge of the text and a soundly based interpretation of it. Mere imagination will not gain credit in textual study for GCSE English Literature.

- In terms of length of essay, do bear in mind that it is only one of several pieces of coursework and there is no need for a 5,000 word blockbuster. Many essays will exceed 1,000 words; by how much you write depends on the material you wish to present and the advice of your teacher.

# Self-test answers Chapters 1–3

Uncover the plot

Mr Jones goes to bed drunk and the animals all gather in the big barn to hear Old Major speak. The pig tells of the misery Man causes animals and preaches Rebellion; finally he relates his dream of a golden future in a song: 'Beasts of England'.

Old Major dies, and the animals continue to hold secret meetings, organised by the pigs, the most intelligent animals. The rebellion is spontaneous; Jones gets drunk again and forgets to feed the animals, so they drive him, his wife and his men off the farm. They burn all the reins, bits, whips and knives, and enter the farmhouse with fear. Snowball changes the name of the farm on the gate and writes up the 7 Commandments. The hay harvest is the best ever and all summer the animals are happy. On Sundays there is no work and their flag is hoisted – a white horn and hoof on a green background. Snowball sums up the commandments as: 'four legs good, two legs bad', which the sheep repeat endlessly. He and Napoleon disagree about everything. Napoleon takes 9 puppies away to educate them secretly. Apples and milk are reserved for the pigs.

Who? What? Why? When? Where? How?

1 Snowball, Napoleon and Squealer, from the teachings of Old Major (2)
2 The cat (1)
3 They gallop right round the farm (2)
4 Manor Farm (2)
5 Because Jones, drunk again, neglects to feed the animals. They help themselves; when the farmer realises, he and his men lash out at them with whips (2)
6 Because every animal helps to its best ability (3)
7 On Midsummer's Day (2)
8 On the end wall of the big barn (2)
9 Jones lets off his gun, thinking that the noise of the animals' singing means there is a fox in the yard (1)
10 'Man is the only real enemy we have…What then must we do? Why, work night and day, body and soul, for the overthrow of the human race!' (1)

Who is this?

1 Benjamin (1)
2 Squealer (2)
3 Boxer (3)
4 Napoleon (3)
5 Mollie (1)
6 Old Major (1)
7 Napoleon (2)
8 Moses the raven (2)
9 Jones (2)
10 Snowball (2)

A question of style

1 The first sentence of the novel contains only one three-syllable word 'remember'. It tells us that Jones is a drunk and establishes the name of the farm
2 The words are simple enough for a very young child to understand, but the combination of words makes no sense at all. Equality is equality – there can be no more or less

3   Orwell's comic touches are nearly always understated in this novel – he moves quickly on from the ludicrous burial of the hams (once pigs) to other matters
4   Something 'commanded' cannot be 'spontaneous'; the animals are under the hand of Napoleon's manipulation
5   Note the brevity of the words used and the simplicity of the sentence structures. The repetition ('again and again') gives an idea of the barrage of shooting. The fatalities are described with brutal clarity, and Napoleon's chipped tail is treated in the same deadpan manner. Orwell slips in the fact that Napoleon, unlike Snowball, keeps to the back of the fighting. 'Directing operations from the rear' ironically reveals him as preserving his own skin

As easy as ABC
1   Mollie's vanity is revealed in the fact that she will only learn the letters of her name, although she is obviously intelligent enough to achieve more.
2   Clover learns all the letters but cannot put them together. She similarly sees the events which occur in Animal Farm, but cannot put the pieces together to make a whole
3   Boxer has 'a somewhat stupid appearance.' He can only learn the letters A, B, C and D, although he works hard at learning the others. Throughout the novel he sticks stubbornly and blindly to what he knows
4   Benjamin can read as well as the pigs, but is as cynical about this as he is about everything else, declaring that there is nothing worth reading. The two occasions when he uses his skill are important; firstly, he reads the legend on the knacker's van to try and help his friend Boxer; and secondly, he reads the last remaining Commandment for Clover, whose usual interpreter, Muriel, has died. Orwell perhaps has some sympathy with Benjamin's contempt for the written word, so often manipulated by the pigs
5   Muriel can read well (she learns from bits of newspaper picked up from the rubbish heap). It is implied that she does not intelligently consider the meaning of what she reads

Prove it!
1   '…a brood of ducklings which had lost their mother, filed into the barn, cheeping feebly and wandering from side to side to find some place where they would not be trodden on. Clover made a sort of wall round them with her great foreleg, and the ducklings nestled down inside it and promptly fell asleep.'
2   'His answer to every problem, every setback, was "I will work harder!" – which he had adopted as his personal motto.'
3   '(Mollie) had taken a piece of blue ribbon from Mrs Jones' dressing table, and was holding it against her shoulder and admiring herself in the glass in a very foolish manner.'
4   'Mollie, it was true, was not good at getting up in the mornings, and had a way of leaving work early on the ground that there was a stone in her hoof.'
5   'When asked whether he was not happier now that Jones was gone, he would say only "Donkeys live a long time. None of you has ever seen a dead donkey"…'

■ Self-test answers Chapters 4–7

Uncover the plot
The fame of Animal Farm grows and, in particular, its song. In October, the pigeons bring news that Jones is leading an attack. He is defeated with only one

animal killed. Snowball and Boxer are given medals for bravery. Mollie is the first animal to desert the farm. The frequent disagreements between Snowball and Napoleon reach a climax over the defence of the windmill. The animals are swept away by Snowball's eloquent pleading, but are prevented from voting for him by Napoleon's dogs who chase him away. Napoleon now assumes power and abolishes debates. Three weeks later, he announces that the windmill will be built after all, over two/three/four years. Boxer works the hardest in this task. Mr Whymper is appointed to act as an intermediary in trading with humans. In November, a storm destroys the windmill and building begins again. Food is scarce and eggs are sold to acquire it; meanwhile Snowball is blamed for everything that goes wrong.

Who? What? Why? When? Where? How?

1   Mollie, because she craves the luxuries and admiration humans provide (5)
2   Boxer (5)
3   The Fourth: 'No animal shall sleep in a bed' (6)
4   He urinates over them, thereby indicating his disgust and contempt for them (5)
5   Against a contract by which Napoleon arranges to sell their eggs (7)
6   He realises its power as a rallying cry (7)
7   Twice a year (October 12th, the anniversary of the Battle of the Cowshed and Midsummer Day, the anniversary of the Rebellion) (4)
8   On the Knoll, the place from which the animals looked out over their property after expelling Jones (5)
9   By a storm. (Napoleon claims that Snowball is responsible) (6)
10 By pigeon (4)

Who is this?

1   Clover (7)
2   Mollie (5)
3   Benjamin (5)
4   Snowball (5)
5   Snowball (7)

Who said that?

1   Snowball (4)
2   Squealer (5)
3   Boxer (7)
4   Squealer (6)

The Seven Commandments

1   The Fourth: 'No animal shall sleep in a bed' (2)
2   They add the words 'with sheets' (6)
3   He says that 'A bed merely means a place to sleep in. A pile of straw in a stall is a bed, properly regarded. The rule was against sheets, which are a human invention.' (6)
4   The Sixth: 'No animal shall kill any other animal' The superiority of the pigs erodes the idea of animals' equality (the Seventh Commandment), while the trade with humans goes against the First: 'Whatever goes upon two legs is an enemy' (8)
5   Four commandments are altered by the pigs, numbers Four, Five, Six and Seven. These become:
    No animal shall sleep in a bed *with sheets* (6)
    No animal shall drink alcohol *to excess* (8)
    No animal shall kill any other animal *without cause* (8)
    All animals are equal *but some are more equal than others* (10)

In addition, the first two commandments, which were condensed by Snowball into 'Four legs good, two legs *bad*' (3) become 'Four legs good, two legs *better*' by the end of the novel.

Prove it!

1   '(The dogs) kept close to Napoleon. It was noticed that they wagged their tails to him in the same way as the other dogs had been used to do to Mr Jones.' (5)

2   'So "Beasts of England" was heard of no more. In its place, Minimus, the poet, had composed another song which began:
    "Animal Farm, Animal Farm,
    Never through me shalt thou come to harm!"
    … But somehow neither the words nor the tune ever seemed to the animals to come up to "Beasts of England" '. (7)

3   'Rumours of a wonderful farm, where the human beings had been turned out and the animals managed their own affairs, continued to circulate in vague and farms, and throughout that year a wave of rebelliousness ran through the countryside.' (4)

4   When it is announced that there will be no more debates:
    'Four young porkers in the front row uttered shrill squeals of disapproval, and all four of them sprang to their feet and began speaking at once.' (5)
    'The four young pigs who had protested when Napoleon abolished the Meetings raised their voices timidly, but they were promptly silenced by a tremendous growling from the dogs' (6)

■ Self-test answers Chapters 8–10

Uncover the plot

Napoleon continues to become less accessible; he plays Pilkington and Frederick against each other over the proposed sale of timber, and is enraged when he discovers he has been tricked. Frederick attacks the farm and destroys the windmill with gunpowder. Six animals are killed but the humans are defeated. To celebrate, the pigs drink whisky. Boxer has injured his hoof but is due to retire on his twelfth birthday. Rations are reduced and Animal Farm becomes a Republic. Boxer collapses and is sold to the slaughterhouse by the pigs, who hold a memorial banquet in his honour. Years pass and the farm grows richer. Few of the animals remember life before the rebellion and they still have pride in their farm; this is destroyed when the pigs begin to walk on their hind legs. Only one of the commandments remain and in the final scene, pigs and humans are shown at a party. Animal Farm is now to be called Manor Farm. When the pigs and men start to argue together, they become indistinguishable from each other.

Who? What? Why? When? Where? How?

1   His nine dogs and a black cockerel, acting as a trumpeter (8)

2   Napoleon and Pilkington, because they both play an ace of spades in the card game – one of them is cheating (10)

3   A whip (10)

4   Another crate of whisky (9)

5   Perhaps he has prior knowledge of Frederick's plan. It suits Napoleon for the animals to be tied up in exhausting physical labour because they have less time to think about their situation (8)

6 Curiosity (10)
7 In April (9)
8 In the farmhouse (10)
9 Twice: once after the storm and once after it is destroyed by Frederick
10 Fifteen (8)

Who is this?
1 Pilkington (10)
2 Mr Whymper (10)
3 Squealer (8)
4 Squealer (9)
5 Squealer (8)
6 Benjamin (10)

Who writes?
1 Pilkington (8)
2 Squealer (10)
3 Minimus (8)
4 The pigs (10)

Taking sides

1 'Good' Characters	'Bad' Characters
Old Major	Mollie
Bluebell	Moses
Jessie	Napoleon
Pitcher	Squealer
Boxer	Minimus
Clover	
Muriel	
Benjamin	
Snowball	

2 Notably, the sheep. Many other animals, though, are not named (for example, the hens and ducks) and do not therefore achieve the individuality that names convey
3 Clover, Benjamin, Moses the raven and a number of the pigs
4 The cat. She is capable of taking care of herself and her own interests. She also typifies the wilder animals, whom it is not possible to indoctrinate. (3)

Prove it!
1 When Boxer collapses, Benjamin '…lay down at Boxer's side, and, without speaking, kept the flies off him with his long tail.' (9)
2 When Boxer is in pain with his split hoof, he only admits it to Clover. 'Clover treated the hoof with poultices of herbs which she prepared by chewing them'
3 'They all declared contemptuously that his stories about Sugarcandy Mountain were lies, and yet they allowed him to remain on the farm, not working, with an allowance of a gill of beer a day.' (9)
4 'Four dogs guarded his bed at night, one at each corner, and a young pig named Pinkeye was given the task of tasting all his food before he ate it, lest it should be poisoned.' (8)
5 Squealer spends a week with them in private, 'teaching them to sing a new song' and when the pigs first appear walking on their hindlegs, the sheep, 'as though at a signal' bleat repeatedly: 'Four legs good, two legs better!'